S0-AAL-039

MUSIC

EXPERIENCES IN EARLY CHILDHOOD

HOLT, RINEHART and WINSTON

New York Chicago
San Francisco Atlanta
Dallas Montreal
Toronto London
Sydney

Editor: Roth Wilkofsky
Project Editor: Ellen Small
Copy Editor: Helen Edersheim
Production Manager: Nancy Myers
Art Director: Louis Scardino
Text Design: Ron Farber
Cover Design: Albert D'Agostino
Text Illustration: Ed Malsberg
Page Makeup: Publishing Synthesis, Ltd.

Library of Congress Cataloging in Publication Data

Andress, Barbara.
    Music experiences in early childhood.

    Bibliography: p.
    Includes index.
        1.   School music—Instruction and study.
    2.   Nursery schools—Music.   I.   Title.
    MT1.A71   372.8'7   97–26605
    ISBN 0–03–021771–9

Copyright © 1980 by Holt, Rinehart and Winston
All rights reserved
Printed in the United States of America
        0123 039 987654321

Acknowledgments

"ABC," "Dance in the Circle," "For Children, Vol. I, No. XXXII" (B. Bartok), "Little Jack Horner—Little Miss Muffet," "Teddy Bear," and "Whosery Here?" from Exploring Music series, by E. Boardman, B. Landis, and B. Andress. © 1975 by Holt, Rinehart and Winston. Used by permission.

"Aija, Anzit, Aija" ("Lullaby My Jamie"): As appears in the publication entitled Folk Lullabies; Copyright © 1969 Oak Publications; All rights reserved; Used by permission.

"Andrew Mine, Jasper Mine," words translated by C.K. Offer. Reprinted from Three Moravian Carols by P. Tate, by permission of Oxford University Press.

"Brow Bender," "Nose Fun" (My Mother and Your Mother"), "See-saw, Margery Daw," and "Shoe a Little Horse," taken from The Annotated Mother Goose with an introduction and notes by William S. Baring-Gould and Ceil Baring-Gould. Copyright © 1962 by William S. and Ceil Baring-Gould. Used by permission of Crown Publishers, Inc.

"Bye Baby Bunting," and "Shanghai Chicken," from 150 American Folk Songs (Erdei-Komlos). © Copyright 1974 by Boosey & Hawkes, Inc. Reprinted by permission.

"Clap Your Hands" and "Down Came a Lady," from American Folk Songs for Children by Ruth Crawford Seeger. Copyright 1948 by Ruth Seeger. Reprinted by permission of Doubleday & Company, Inc.

"Hickory, Dickory, Dock" from The Spectrum of Music, Teacher's Annotated Edition of Kindergarten Book. M.V. Marsh, C. Rinehart, E. Savage. Macmillan Publishing Co., Inc. Copyright © 1974. Used by permission.

"How Many Days Has My Baby to Play" "Johnny, Get Your Hair Cut," "Knock at the Door," and "Where is Thumbkin?" from Music for Early Childhood, New Dimensions in Music, R. Choate, L. Kjelson, R. Berg, E. Troth. Used by permission of American Book Company, 130 West 50th Street, New York, New York 10020

"I Went to the River," adapted from the folk lyrics in H. Courlander, Negro Folk Music U.S.A., New York: Columbia University Press, 1963 by permission of the publisher.

"Michael Finnegan," from The Fireside Book of Children's Songs. Copyright © 1966 by Marie Winn and Allen Miller. Reprinted by permission of Simon & Schuster, a Division of Gulf & Western Corporation.

"Shake That Little Foot" and "The Old Gray Cat" from Silver Burdett Music Early Childhood © 1976 by Silver Burdett Company. Reprinted by permission.

Material on the sound box originally appeared in a different form in Music in Early Childhood (Music Educators National Conference, 1973) which was prepared by the MENC National Commission on Instruction, with the author as Chairman of the Early Childhood Committee. Used by permission.

Sound Paddle from "Inside Sounds," Exploring Music, Kindergarten, E. Boardman, B. Landis, B. Andress. © 1975 Holt, Rinehart and Winston. Used by permission.

The mushroom bell games are summarized from Developing the Senses, Anna Marie Maccheroni, © 1950, World Library Publication. Reprinted with permission.

Preface

This book presents a program of music experiences for young children which, in contrast to many traditional ones, focuses on process, not necessarily on product. The program embodies a hands-on, experiential discovery approach to music, rather than imposing ideas and repertoire on the child. An overstructured music program imposed from without merely encourages children very early in life to let others think for them. On the other hand, early experiences can set a pattern through which children themselves learn, explore, choose, and make judgments about ways in which they will use and enjoy music throughout their lives. Such experiences are the goal of this book.

This book is intended to serve the needs of those who work with young children: early-childhood specialists in public and private schools; teachers in such child developmental programs as those in home economics and education departments; music educators; and parents. Along with understanding the growth and development of the child, a music educator must understand the preschool setting and the methods for planning sequential music growth. I have attempted to integrate information about all of these aspects of the education process so that for each activity the reasoning, in terms of child development, is explicit. Further, this book provides insights into learning styles of the three- to five-year-old child. To this end, observations of children learning through play activity are included throughout the text.

The early-childhood specialist's personal growth in music skills also is important. I have therefore included a chapter for adults on playing instruments and developing a greater range of vocal skill.

To create a program for children three to five years old, we must deal with the young child's mind and limited ability to use language or other abstract means of communication. We must rely on observation and personal interpretation to determine the nature and quality of learning that is taking place. Attempting to understand the thought processes and developmental path of the very young child is often difficult and sometimes even humbling. Yet, if we do not make the attempt, we lose the opportunity to provide direction, the opportunity to influence early behaviors that will affect the child's view of the world throughout life.

In developing the material in this book, I have relied on both my own research and the research of others. I have carried out my research over a period of six years in direct contact with children aged three to five. During this period of study, my main concern has been to shape a program that deals sequentially with concepts basic to the understanding of music. The program as presented here comes from that involvement and also incorporates the findings of learning theorists, experienced music educators, and early-childhood specialists.

Special Acknowledgments

Many people have contributed in a variety of ways to this publication. I wish to give special thanks to Hope Heimann for ideas in movement; Harold Collier for construction of prototype instruments and sound studies; Arizona State University undergraduate and graduate students who have fielded ideas and contributed observations of children learning; Peggy Brokaw and other classroom teachers who worked daily with the girls and boys in the Arizona State University Child Developmental Laboratory; and the reviewers who provided invaluable assistance in refining the final copy: Clifford D. Alper, Towson State University, Virginia D. Austin, State University College at Buffalo, Dr. Amy L. Brown, Florida State University, Dr. Ruth De Cesare, Indiana University of Pennsylvania, Jo Faulmann, Illinois State University, Russell M. Harrison, San Jose State University, Eunice B. Meske, The University of Wisconsin-Madison, Sharon Mitchell, College Conservatory of Music, University of Cincinnati, Sally Monsour, Georgia State University, and Claire Nanis, University of Delaware.

Contents

The Child-Centered Music Program

How fortunate we are

And privileged to be

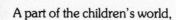

A part of the children's world,

To see what they see.

"To see what they see" is the clue for the teacher of young children. The educational process begins with the child. Threes cannot yet adequately verbalize feelings and understandings; thus, we must attempt to see as they see, to follow their lead. Only through careful observation can we gain insight into how the three- to five-year-old child views the world and then find ways to make an impact on what is to be learned and how the child is to learn it.

The Three does not think and react like the Four; the Four is not able to think nearly so logically as the Five. Nor do children of this age group think like adults, for among their many limitations is the inability to perceive sequence, even though they are in the process of formulating ideas that suggest cause and effect. The experiences at the early stages of this developmental span must be thought of as single-focus, "one-dimensional" activities, not necessarily leading immediately to the next step as it might be perceived by the adult.

Child-centered experiences most effectively stimulate growth in understanding because they are appropriate for the particular mode of learning and scope of comprehension at a given time. When dealing with very young children, one has no alternative other than the child-centered approach, for this is a chronological age of notable egocentricity. Children's awareness is centered completely on themselves and that part of the world they have elected to utilize.

The child's development requires multiple experiences in placing things in order by sight and sound. Many experiences with cause-and-effect activities are needed to bring about an understanding of sequence and logic. Music education at this level must place priority on exploratory experiences and less emphasis on amassing a repertoire of song and game activities.

The youngest of children respond to beauty. A child-centered music program must use the finest examples of music representing many styles of various cultures in time. The sounds that children work with should be such that the esthetic experience is an integral part of their earliest encounters.

Process

An intensive program of seeing, hearing, and doing in children's early years will significantly affect their later ability to use abstract symbols. The music program for the three- to five-year-old must establish a solid experiential base so that any symbols, like language or music notation, are imposed only after the child has encountered and perceived that which is to be labeled. When learning about music, the child will act in these ways:

1. Explore by playing at random with sounds (assimilating and accommodating tasks);
2. Play by manipulating more organized soundmaking and musical materials (more complex accommodating tasks);
3. Formulate ideas about sounds (early discriminating tasks);
4. Develop simple concepts about sounds and their relationships (grading, ordering, classifying tasks);
5. Exert power over media (organizing, improvising, and recalling tasks);
6. Define sounds by words and symbols (conceptualizing, abstracting tasks).

Implementation of this approach places responsibility upon the teacher and parent to create musical learning environments that arouse the child's curiosity. Refinements and changes in each environment are made as a result of observing the responses of the learner in action. The adult serves the child by observing and then by acting to clarify, label, model, or motivate experiences. The adult observer must be able to minimize concerns for the product and to focus on the process with which the child is involved.

A child-centered music program has these characteristics:

1. The child is involved in a sensory-motor approach to learning.
2. The child is in control of his learning.
3. The child makes choices about what is to be learned from an environment rich in musical resources.
4. The child deals with musical ideas through play and manipulation of materials.
5. The child interacts independently or socially with music depending on the stage of development.

6. The child operates in an environment in which the teacher or parent actively participates by intervening to motivate action and construct musical problems to be solved.

A Developmental Program

If the child is not yet ready to understand that one idea leads to another, is it necessary to consider a developmental music program for early childhood? Would not the child grow as effectively if allowed merely to assimilate musical sounds normally in the environment? Need more be offered than the opportunity to sing or move to music? Consideration of these questions may suggest an approach in which the child is allowed to grow naturally and unaided during this stage. Research has indicated, however, that these are crucial learning years for the child, a time for perceiving and formulating ideas about the world.

Dr. Benjamin Bloom of the University of Chicago has stated that 80 percent of all learning at age seventeen has been acquired by eight years of age, and indeed 50 percent of that by age four. He adds that academic interest appears before the eighth year. During this time, the child is acquiring language at a rapid rate, and language is indicative of emerging thought. As this is an age of such rapid development, music too, must be a significant part of the learning environment and must be presented in a logical order if it is to become part of a child's life. Further, research indicates that learning processes inherent in musical activities reflect basic human needs, that perhaps music should not be thought of as useful only as a beautiful, sensitizing experience for children. It may indeed be basic to all learning.

Our traditional approach, involving children in large group settings where they listen, play, sing, and move to heritage music materials, can no longer represent the sole mode of learning. This approach should be but one part of a larger program in which children interact and make decisions about sounds, their quality, intensity, pitch, and duration. The children should manipulate and play with sounds, musical and environmental, as a means to ordering and organizing their musical world.

Learning Through Play

The child moves, senses, and vocalizes as he acts upon his world.[1] Children must explore with every sense; they must feel, taste, smell, see, and hear. They must test their power over objects: How loud will a sound be? How hard can an object be struck? Can it be shaken or squeezed to create a sound? How high or how fast can it be made to move?

Through play, the child imitates persons and objects in an effort to sort, piece together, and understand many different ideas. The fluid manner in which the child's mind moves between fantasy and reality makes play a very real learning experience. Play involves

[1]For the sake of simplicity only, we sometimes use the masculine generic pronouns; they should always be understood to mean either sex.

decision-making, planning, and controlling situations, all important processes in the child's growth.

Children experiment with body movement to give shape to musical sounds. They "talk" with their bodies, expressing ideas and emotions for which they do not yet have language symbols. They learn how they "fit" in space through the use of exploratory movement involving front, behind, up, down, to the side.

The child learns through play that centers first on self, secondarily on things and other persons. Through play, the child builds a self-image.

Play as a mode of learning has not always been taken seriously by those responsible for the education of children. In earlier times, play was often viewed as an interruption of education's major concern—perfecting important work skills and understandings. Play was allowed for young children but rarely considered a vital learning tool.

Many of today's educators valiantly attempt to promote a "learn through play" philosophy at the kindergarten level. The result too often is that parental and even peer pressures turn play-based curriculums into watered-down first-grade programs. In this situation, the child acquires minimal reading skills, ability to count to a certain number, and perhaps, on a limited basis, the ability to read and respond to traditional music notation. The uninformed adult is then reassured that learning has indeed taken place because the child can successfully parrot this knowledge. One of the most significant ways in which the child learns is through imitation, but imitation without understanding merely promotes a conditioned response that may fool observers into believing that true learning has taken place.

The child who is introduced to symbols before being involved in such comparable hands-on experiences as manipulating, sorting, and sequencing usually resorts to rote learning. While able to echo words, count to ten, or read a rhythm pattern, the child too often fails to understand the meaning of the response. Through environmental play, the child encounters and manipulates objects representing specific ideas; later, the symbols are applied.

Children of three to five years intellectually enter this stage with limited skills. Through a sensory-motor approach to learning, they rapidly evolve from the more concrete to the abstract stage, in which the power of symbolic language and the concepts inherent therein provide skills for more efficient ways to deal with the world.

Young Children at Play

Twos

Children at two like to be with other children although they do not play cooperatively. Their play involves mother-child games. They love to feel, pound, or squeeze toys that produce sounds or motion. Drum banging is most gratifying, since the loud sounds make children feel in full control of their environment. They greatly enjoy games of touching fingers and toes while rhythmically chanting.

The two-year-old plays with language, often repetitively; thus, simple rhymes are formulated. Repetition of the same song, chant or play activity is a favorite experience. This child moves by swaying, swinging arms, clapping hands, and bouncing torso. Adult observers may have the delightful experience of watching an improvised dance in front of the television or phonograph in which the child bobs or bounces to the music with little movement through space. The rhythms do not necessarily follow the basic beat of the music, and the motions may be awkward, but the body is definitely responding with joyful exuberance to the musical sounds. The child is already demonstrating the ability to discriminate between musical and non-musical sounds in the environment.

Threes

Threes play in the company of others, not necessarily cooperatively. Sharing begins to enter, reluctantly. The child works hard to acquire language. Imaginative play begins to reflect language and logic. Imagination is often bound to what has most recently been seen and has caught the child's interest. This child speaks and sings thoughts aloud, but language is not necessarily used as a conversational tool. Sounds and words express feelings and actions. The playful repetition of word patterns becomes a delightful song game, and the child often makes up simple chants to accompany various play activities.

The Three moves in a more coordinated manner than the Two, often reflecting fairly accurate rhythmic responses. This child uses much energy in movement, falling and tumbling down, yet exerting some controls if he deems it important to do so.

When nearing four, the child discovers it is fun to have a friend with whom to talk and play. Through limited experiences, the Three develops an awareness of and a greater interest in being a part of a group.

Fours

Fours exhibit more social behavior. The child is still learning to share, but this is a great time for a friend. Individual exploration and discovery must still be provided so that the child may work with self-chosen materials at a self-chosen rate.

The Four is growing in ability to see relationships and can be quite successful in ordering and classifying sounds. Games involving simple tonal and timbre discrimination tasks are of great interest. Children this age are capable of organizing sounds to help express a story or accompany a song. They are beginning to remember sequence and greatly enjoy dramatization; they listen with sustained interest.

Fours talk a great deal with much exaggeration. Songs with nonsense words, silly language, and rhyming are favorites. As the children become more involved with the group, it becomes more important to them to match the tones of others when singing. Thus, matching tones is a growing skill for the Fours. Their movement activities are also becoming more accurate.

Fives

Fives are more able to cope with group experiences. They play both independently and socially when exploring and performing music. Their growing ability to reverse a trend of thought is demonstrated by the ability to repeat simple musical patterns. Fives are more aware of multiple sounds played simultaneously, and they can respond with greater accuracy to the basic beat. They possess greater skill in matching tones of others when singing. The Five can begin to use visual ikons[2] representing musical sound and is growing in ability to improvise, organize, recall, and reorganize sounds or musical ideas.

Five-year-olds speak conversationally with others, question to seek information. As yet, they have not totally separated fantasy and reality; their play still involves much imagination.

Limited movement requiring a sense of balance is now possible. The adult can expect more rhythmic accuracy reflecting the child's higher degree of muscle control.

Summary

A music program for the three- to five-year-old child must be child-centered. Musical growth comes about through an experiential, learn-through-play approach. The adult serves to set the learning environment and to assist the child in labeling and understanding that which is encountered.

---

[2]"Ikon" is a term used by Jerome Bruner to indicate a presymbolic stage wherein the child is internalizing an object or sound and can thus retain an image of it when it is no longer present. The ikon is a device to help the child internalize. Music educators employ such devices when they use a long or short line to indicate sound duration.

The Learning Environment

The child drinks in the environment
just as if drinking milk.
Large gulps
end
in a

wide mustache
The child licks here and there
before SWIPING it away
with the back of the hand.

Children make their greatest progress when they are curious about their environment. Questions of "why" need to be motivated so that the learner is fulfilling a personal need to find answers rather than having information that may or may not seem relevant imposed upon him.

Settings that arouse a child's interest should be considered by the curriculum planner of the preschool child's day.

The viable preschool classroom provides easy access by children to the various areas of learning. The following plan shows a possible physical organization of the room.

Room organization is a key to motivating the child's choice of activities. Notice that on entering the room, the child immediately sees learning materials on the tables. The teacher hopes to arouse the child's interest and thus involvement in these preset learning experiences. Individual participation in these learning areas still depends on free choice. The table area houses such problem-solving

The Preschool Classroom

manipulative materials as puzzles, paper, paste, clay, or soundmakers. Objects for nature and science studies are also available in this area.

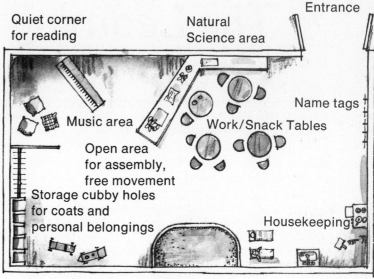

Quiet corner for reading

Natural Science area

Entrance

Music area

Name tags

Work/Snack Tables

Open area for assembly, free movement

Storage cubby holes for coats and personal belongings

Housekeeping

Small wheel toys

Wet area, Sand, Painting

The teacher greets the children each day when they first enter the room. A routine is established: a name tag is identified by each child, perhaps with the help of the teacher, and then pinned to the child's clothing. The teacher aide is seated in the area where exploratory materials are displayed. Children are greeted by the aide, and their questions and distant or close participation begin. (A child may be participating when viewing from a distance as well as when actually engaged in a hands-on activity.)

In a typical preschool, the first hour of the day is a time of individual interaction with self-chosen activities. This hour may be followed by a period outdoors, during which the child is still learning through play. Many music activities can be included in outdoor experiences. When children return to the classroom, it is snack time. Children serve themselves and sometimes help others by pouring juice and passing crackers. This is another important learning time. During it, the adult may lead a discussion, picking up cues from the children's interests of the moment, or prepare the group for the next activity. After snack time, large groups form for "play together" experiences.

Within this environment, children use music as a part of their normal play fantasy. The following observations, noted over a period of time and with different groups, provide insight into how three- and four-year-old children operate within the classroom setting and subconsciously incorporate music into their activities.

On this particular day there were four areas of activity:

- a puzzle table with one child and an adult;
- another work table with pegboard where another child was engrossed for a long period of time;
- the playdough table where two children worked for a short time;
- a table where many of the group were with the teacher rolling out bread dough, spreading it with butter, and sprinkling on sugar and cinnamon.

Karen was in the housekeeping area, dressed up with heels, bracelets, long dress, and oversized beads. As she clomped around in her heels she sang a "la-la-la" tune over and over, jiggling her beads to the music. She rocked in a chair and then went to the cradle, continuing to sing her "la-la-la" sounds with each rocking motion. She stopped abruptly and went to a shelf where she found a carton full of objects. She proceeded to comb her hair and look at herself in the mirror, saying, "I got lots of stuff!" She picked up a doll, giggled, and handed it to Rodney, who was now rocking the chair. She moved to the sink, saying, "I'm the sister," and then washed dishes for an instant. Next, she covered up a child who had decided to "scrunch up" and be the baby in the doll bed. The "baby" ordered her to stop. She learned that it was now her turn at the dough table, so in all her dress-up clothes, she clomped to the work area, again singing "la-la-la."

At the table, she rolled out her dough and patted it several times. She was very interested in the activity and didn't participate in any conversation. She tasted the mixture several times by licking her sticky fingers. The teacher was telling some children that they had forgotten not to run in the room and that they might have to sit down. Karen replied (with a better solution), "Or else they'll have to go outside and run." No one came to show Karen how to roll the dough for some time, so she sat patiently. Finally, an adult helped her. After she had completed her job, she ate a couple of the rolls uncooked.

Julie put on a pair of rain boots and strutted around the room, singing, "I'm going out in the rain . . . now I'm walking in the water . . . I like my dolly in the rain." An entire rain story was told and dramatized in song.

One boy announced that he wanted to play the piano. The teacher quickly responded, "I'll help you play the piano." Several other children, including Julie, were attracted by the activity. The children played "Old Black Witch," with fingers making awesome sounds on the lower part of the piano. Julie crowded in and timidly played one key repeatedly while softly humming to herself. She seemed quite oblivious to the other children's exciting story. The activity became somewhat chaotic with all the children attempting to add ideas. Julie withdrew. The teacher intervened to help redirect ideas and restore calm. The children were soon satisfied with their sound story and moved to other areas of the room.

Children were busy at the work table pasting tissue-paper pictures. During the morning, almost every child had participated in the activity without any adult intervention. Making a picture took five to ten minutes at the most, and when one was completed, it was displayed on the bulletin board.

There were three or four boys of bounding energy who quickly finished their pictures. They became the nomads of the class, drifting from one activity to another, finding nothing in which they wanted to become involved. They seemed to derive their greatest delight from bumping into each other, letting their fireman hats hit the floor, or plowing through another boy's carefully arranged railroad track. Shoving and exchanging taunts were the only prerequisites needed to invite a quarrel, but it was usually short-lived since their attention was easily distracted. Running and two-foot hopping were their favorite modes of moving. David soon tired of the antics of the group and was content to watch the children using playdough. He displayed great originality in "sitting" in his chair. He began by balancing on the two back legs and then discovered that he could make it wobble with little effort. If he wasn't wiggling, he was kicking his feet aimlessly in the air or hanging over the back of his chair like a rag doll. He culminated his chair gymnastics by pushing himself backwards in short jerks across the room.

He then asked the name of a child seated nearby. The boy answered, "Jason." David followed the boy's answer with a rhythm chant: "Your name is J, Jack, Jumbo!" and with a screech, ended with "Jack in the box!" He then jumped up and down across the room shouting, "Jump! Jump! Jump!"

During snack time the children were interested in talking about the seeds they had just planted and how long it would be before the plants appeared. Teacher was a part of the discussion group and at an opportune time told the children that when they finished their snack she would have a story for everyone. The children began to gather on the rug for the promised story. It was quite simple, with felt figures used to guide the action. The story told of three little ghosts and how they had run home one at a time because they feared either a witch or a goblin. The children asked to hear the story again and again; at the third reading, they were invited to play the parts, which they most enthusiastically did.

The teacher then changed to another activity. Now, the children were going to play the **name game,** adding what they would be for Halloween. At this time the children began the following chant, clapping a steady beat for accompaniment:

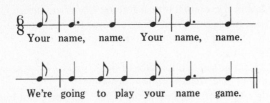

Your name, name. Your name, name.

We're going to play your name game.

After this part was chanted, each child was to add in rhythm, "My name is (Billie), and I'll be a (skeleton)."

Sharon knew the chant for the **name game** and said it in a soft voice along with the group. She also clapped her hands but not in time with the chant. This, however, seemed unimportant to her. When her turn came to give her name, she said it more loudly and excitedly than did the other children: "My name is *Sharon,* and I'm going to be a *lion!*"

Communicating with Children

Communicating with children, helping them to verbalize their feelings and understandings, is the adult responsibility in the preschool classroom. The questioning and testing child is the one who is learning. All conversations, questions, answers within the learning environment, whether child-initiated or motivated by the teacher, are important.

To help the child communicate, the following techniques are useful:

1. Stop what you are doing; listen with interest.
2. Do not tower over children. Sit or stoop, eliciting eye-to-eye contact.
3. Do not be overly quick to disagree; hear the child out.
4. Show you are interested by accepting and acknowledging how the child feels.
5. Speak words of encouragement (teachers are acceptors, not critics or producers).
6. Do not talk down to or at the child. Discuss intelligently with him.
7. Do not subject the child to wordy sermons or lengthy lectures.
8. Be consistent in what you say you will do; use a quiet, firm voice.
9. Do not lift or carry the child, even when asked to do so. Maintain the idea that the child is independently operating. Hug or comfort with the child's feet always on the ground.

It is sometimes necessary to deal with unacceptable behavior. This can be done in a number of ways:

1. State positively what you want the child to do. When you attempt to thwart an undesirable action, "Johnny, don't step on the drum!" is ineffective, for all Johnny hears is ". . . step on the drum!" A positive comment states what you want the child to do: "Johnny, pick up the drum and place it on the table."

2. Channel the child's interest away from unwanted behavior to a new, more positive action (change the subject).
3. If the child persists in arguing, attempt to involve him in an agreement:
"As long as we can talk about this, I will be happy to continue, but right now we are getting nowhere."
"We have both said what we think. I'm sorry but we just don't agree."

The teacher will develop a variety of techniques for working with children based on observing how each child deals with individual problems. The knowledge of how the child copes provides cues for circumventing undersirable actions before the situation evolves into a negative confrontation.

Music Environments in the Preschool

Music environments are structured much like the other learning settings in the preschool. Just as there is a special housekeeping area, there is a special music area; just as there are curricular manipulative materials at the work tables, there are problem-solving sound studies, too. Music and movement need open space. This should be available near the record player, tape recorder, piano, or other instruments. The child is provided with a rich assortment of ways to encounter music on a self-choice or guided basis throughout the daily classroom experiences.

Music environments may be sophisticated or quite simple, depending upon the imagination, energy, physical space, and resources available to the teacher. Teachers of young children are generally masters of improvisation when it comes to acquiring materials for learning. They cut, paste, saw, hammer, collect, and store in order to devise effective learning environments. Other people's discards become treasures to these teachers. It has been the author's experience that they need only the germ of an idea to find a way to adapt and provide a setting.

The music environment must attract children to the area. The teacher's objective is to entice the child to come and play. A permanent area assures that the child can operate within the security of predictable materials. Certain musical resources are always available in such a setting—piano, record player or tape recorder, and small percussion instruments. Additional materials used in sound studies may be considered short-term, displayed only as long as the child exhibits interest in them.

A floor plan for the music area can be as diverse as the physical characteristics of the room allow. Bookshelves or piano can serve as dividers to cordon off areas. A large open space should be available for movement. A sound box (see page 91) can create a special place within which to make music. A permanent interest area could include a cassette replay machine placed within child's reach, with a record player nearby for teacher's use. It is not recommended that children be allowed to use the record player, for when they do, machine and recordings soon become impaired. The result is that the children listen to the poor tone quality of very abused recordings on a player that suffers from speed-control or arm damage. Any learning that takes place is not musical but mechanical, for the child is merely manipulating the "stop and go" features of the equipment. The child may easily be taught to use the cassette player, however; it is relatively indestructible and the tape can be played over and over without affecting the tone quality.

Music centers may vary in elaborateness and permanence. Those described here have all proved their usefulness. The reader is encouraged to adapt both the materials and designs of these centers to suit particular learning environments.

Music Centers

THE SOUND BOX

A sound box may become one of the permanent music centers in the room. It consists of a plywood or cardboard box with a removable panel, the sound wall. Wood construction creates a more durable and resonant chamber. The sound box has a lid, floor, and four sides each approximately four feet square.

"Crawl-in holes" in the sides and openings in the lid for light and observation may be cut in free-form designs.

The sound wall is a plywood panel slid in between two thin

strips of wood, which hold it in place. The panel is slightly smaller than a side. It may be adapted for the purpose of a particular sound study. The sound wall can be changed by lifting the lid of the box.

The child's sound studies (see Chapter 5) in the box use large motor movements. Sound explorations involve assimilation of such sounds as buzzing, thudding, or ringing and the use of such different sound starters as mallets, beaters, and fingers.

Inside the Sound Box

THE SOUND NOOK

Enclosures for sound environments need not be constructed to control sound, for that is a complicated and often expensive procedure. Rather, they are used as visual barriers so that the child is not attracted to another activity before satisfactorily exploring the idea at hand.

The child delights in small enclosed spaces in which to imagine and explore. A small soundmaker, like a music box or a bell, may be taken to a private spot created by a grouping of brightly painted cardboard boxes or round cardboard barrels.

THE SOUND CIRCLE OR SPOT

A learning environment may be set by making a circle with masking tape in an open area. Teacher sits within the circle strumming or experimenting with a small percussion instrument.

The child questions, "What're you doing?"

Teacher responds, "I'm sitting in a hole. Do you want to sit in the hole with me?"

This brief inquiry and answer are usually enough to initiate a delightful musical encounter whether singing, listening, playing instruments, or moving to music.

An environment may also be set with "spots." The teacher may initiate the exchange: "You know what I'm doing? I'm sitting on a spot!" Then the teacher moves just a little to show the masking tape X upon which she is sitting. She continues, "Can you find a spot and cover it with your foot? Can you cover it with your finger? Your seat? Nose? Ear?"

"Can you move away from the spot?" Teacher rubs or beats a drum to copy the child's movement (short, jerky, smooth, or even). The game continues: "Can you come back? Find another spot? Another? Can you jump to a spot? Tip-toe? Turn?"

Descriptive sounds coupled with the child's movements make this an exciting game.

THE CARD-TABLE THEATER

A card table can become a theater if a decorated cover is stitched to create sides. The cover consists of sturdy fabric cut and sewn to fit over the table (see illustration). The edges of the door opening are bound off, and drapery weights are placed in the hem. The cover may be decorated by appliquéing designs, using iron-on patches, or drawing with felt pens.

Pictures of the story are put inside the theater. The record player or tape recorder can stand on top of the table or on a nearby table or shelf with the speaker down in the enclosure. In this way, the teacher can control the equipment. As the children may lean on the theater "wall" as they listen, it is best to place one side of the table against the room wall.

THE OPEN PIANO

Children are fascinated by the mechanical movement inside the piano. It is possible to cut windows in the case above the keyboard and insert clear plastic so that children can see the action as the hammers produce sounds.

THE SOUND SCREEN

A variation of the sound box is a portable screen that can be turned to make a music corner or can be placed against a wall. The screen should have two walls, as indicated in the illustration. Again the walls should be about four feet square. A six-inch space between the walls provides resonance and also space for instruments that may be attached to the wall. Wide feet on the screen guard against tipping.

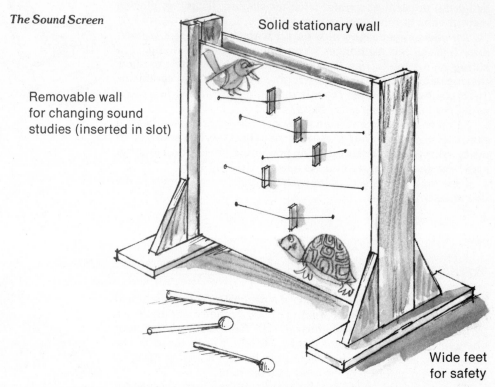

The Sound Screen

Solid stationary wall

Removable wall for changing sound studies (inserted in slot)

Wide feet for safety

Many sound studies are carried out at the work tables. These studies are changed frequently and may or may not need teacher guidance. The child may simply go to the area and play with a sound-matching puzzle.

Seldom is only one child involved in an activity. Children may participate actively or by observing watchfully in any or all of the environmental settings.

Observing Children Learn

The music sound box was placed in the room for the first time. One wall of the box contained various grades of sandpaper for sound exploration. The arriving children could not help noticing the big, brightly painted box. Several of the more aggressive boys were immediately attracted to it. They even had to be reminded to put their coats away before "checking it out." One boy said as he peeked into the hole in the box, "I think I'll go in there." Two others joined in with "Me, too! Me, too!" They quickly discovered the sound starters (mallets, sticks) lying on the floor and immediately made vocal sounds as well as the swishing sounds on the sandpaper wall.

Jennifer arrived that morning very bundled up in her coat and fiercely clutching her teddy bear. No amount of coaxing convinced her to leave her teddy bear in the special place for toys from home, so she was allowed to keep it. In order to hang up her coat, Jennifer had to pass the bright new box. This she did cautiously, making as big a circle around it as space allowed. All through the morning activities Jennifer would pause and look at the box and listen to the sounds emanating from it. However, she continued to clutch her bear and move to other activities.

In the final moments of the day, mothers began arriving to pick up their children. When Jennifer spotted her mother, she again passed the music box going to the closet. She collected her coat and began dragging it and the bear toward her mother. Again she was confronted by the box. Abruptly she turned, dropped both bear and coat, crawled into the box, made three loud swishing sounds, hurried back out of the box, scooped up her bear and coat, and ran to her mother with a broad satisfied grin on her face.

On subsequent days, Jennifer continued to be curious about the sound box. She was soon participating fully as a "sound explorer" in the box.

Three children were striking at random the resonator bells they had found on one of the work tables. They were delighted with the ringing sounds and struggled to strike one another's bells as well as their own. The teacher interceded, talking about taking turns and inserting vocabulary by saying, "Listen to Mary's ringing sound . . . Susie has a ringing sound . . . I hear Johnny's sound go ring-a-ling."

Susie was doing her best to share but managed the group play only briefly. Suddenly, she scooped up one of the bells and a mallet, and sped across the room shouting, "This is my very own sound . . . my very own!"

The Kindergarten Classroom

The physical arrangements of kindergarten classrooms are as varied as the many philosophies, available staff, space, and money among schools. Since the kindergarten is usually housed in a K-8 school plant, specially designated areas are often set aside to accommodate both in-room and outdoor learning environments. The rooms may be adapted from typical public school classrooms or be specially designed for kindergarten needs.

Indoors

The classroom is usually structured much like the preschool room. Interest areas (including music), special-size furniture, and a place for water play are available. More provisions for group-size play areas are included. Centers are established in various areas, and often space is uniquely used. Described below are a few ideas for using physical space in the kindergarten classroom, not necessarily as music environments. The teacher, however, might use any of the areas to introduce appropriate music activities.

1. Within the room, a few cubicles using only half-walls were built. The walls are sturdy, carpeted, and can be used to lean against. Narrow aisles between the cubicles permit traffic flow. The half-walls allow teacher to observe activities while providing a special place for children to work, pretend, or make music. The size of the cubicles is varied to accommodate various group sizes.

2. A sturdy hollow tree trunk was created from a large tube. The tube was attached to both floor and ceiling. A crawl hole was cut in the bottom so that a child could enter and then peek out through various "knotholes" or use a periscope limb for viewing room activities. A few indentations formed small shelves on the outside of the trunk. Various science studies (leaves, bugs) were placed on the tree or in a nearby area.

3. A sunken large-group activity area was part of the permanent room arrangement. Seating was on steps, activities on the lowest level. A minimal lighting system comprising a few colored spots and a dimmer switch was provided for use with dramatizations or expressive movement.

4. A long, low divider screen with "windows" placed at different levels separated areas in the room. The openings were cut into the various shapes children would be studying during the year—circles, rectangles, triangles, squares, and ellipses. Some of the openings had panes made of plastic; others were uncovered.

5. A three-sided screen with plywood panels four feet square provided six settings for imaginative play. The panels were double-hinged so that both sides could be utilized. The screen was folded with two of the standing sides placed in the corner of the room so that only the selected panel was exposed for use. Each painted panel represented a store, airport terminal, puppet stage, office building, or filling station. Doors and window openings were cut into each panel.

Outdoors The outdoor area is ideally directly accessible from the kindergarten classroom. Planners have designed such challenges for children as hills, concrete tunnels, telephone pole clusters, buildings, and tricycle trails with bridges. All these settings lend themselves to much imaginative play. Music can be included very naturally as a part of these environments.

1. Use the bridge to produce an improvised musical of *The Three Billy Goats Gruff.* Sing instead of talking the story. "Who wants to be Big Billy Goat Gruff?"

2. Tubular brass or aluminum chimes can be suspended from a tree limb. Each chime must also be attached to the ground with a string and nail to prevent it from swinging when struck with mallets. The children can explore ringing sounds under the trees.

3. A "singing stump" was so designated where a tree had been cut down. On nice days the Autoharp was placed on the stump for the children's use. The teacher supervised the area as the Autoharp is not a durable outside toy.

The kindergarten curriculum provides many hands-on experiences in science, mathematics, reading, music, and art. A typical weekly schedule is as follows:

Monday — Wednesday — Friday

Arrival
 Time—Selection of puzzles, games, books, or cassette music tapes
 9:00—Circle Time; conversation emphasizing plans for the day's activities
 9:15—Language development program
 9:45—Story Time
 10:15—Activity Centers or Outdoor play
 10:45—Free selection of games, puzzles, music materials
 11:15—Group discussion; day's activities reviewed

Tuesday — Thursday

 9:00—Outdoor play
 9:30—Sharing songs; group music
 9:40—Language development program
 10:10—Rest
 10:15—Rhythms; action songs
 10:30—Art; free play
 11:15—Story Time

Music is integrated into the weekly schedule. It can be correlated with other subjects in meaningful ways in addition to being taught at special times.

As in the preschool program, music for the kindergartener should be an integral part of the curriculum. The major responsibility for guiding music experiences for kindergarten girls and boys will rest on the ever-present classroom teacher, but the teacher may have the assistance and guidance of the music specialist.

Classroom Teacher

The classroom teacher may have total responsibility for the child's musical growth. In the hands of the classroom teacher, music can be a very fluid part of the day's activities. Music experiences cannot be left to chance, however; plans for both individual study and group sessions should be carefully developed with specific objectives in mind.

The teaching of music at this level should not be approached with feelings of insecurity. There are no concepts so difficult that the less skilled musician cannot grow to be comfortable in presenting them to children. Unfortunately, music is often viewed as a highly specialized, almost mystical subject which only a talented few can successfully teach. There is no doubt that the more one knows about a subject the more secure he will be in communicating it to children. In this instance, however, the teacher is asked to model and present only materials appropriate to a very young child. Songs are simple; movements and performance on instruments involve only introductory ideas; musical concepts are no more complex than those encountered in teaching other subjects: "Sounds are long or short, high or low."

The teacher will need these attributes:

1. The conviction that music is important for children;
2. A willingness to improve personal musical skills;
3. A personal excitement about and love of music;
4. The ability to respond to a steady beat or simple rhythm pattern;
5. An in-tune singing voice;
6. The ability to hear differences in sounds;
7. Music materials and resources.

With a blend of common sense and some good basic text guides and recordings, any teacher can provide a solid program for children. Classroom teachers who seek out the many opportunities for professional growth, such as attending music workshops and consulting with music specialists, soon find they have become quite "specialized" themselves.

Music Specialist

The music specialist works within the kindergarten program in various ways determined by other responsibilities to the K-8 school program. The music specialist may be a resource person to the classroom teacher, may serve as a team teacher, or may have major responsibility for the program.

Rarely can a child-centered music program be implemented by the occasional visit of the music specialist. The very nature of the program requires that music be a part of the daily activities. The expertise of the music specialist is most valuable to the classroom teacher; conversely, the classroom teacher has more information about the children and how each individual is learning. A team approach to the teaching of music at this level is highly desirable.

Traditionally, the music specialist schedules the kindergarten classes as one of the many to be taught at the elementary level. Depending on what the schedule will allow, the kindergarten may be allotted time two or three times weekly, or sometimes daily for fifteen or twenty minutes.

Should the schedule permit, a most effective way to use the time of the music specialist is to plan it all in one block. By so doing, the specialist can be in the kindergarten room for an hour or more at one time. During this time, sound studies for the week may be set, work with small groups or individual children may occur, and a twenty-minute session with the total group may be directed. With the week's activities well launched, the classroom teacher can provide musical experiences for the remainder of the week.

If the music teacher is scheduled for twenty-minute classes several times a week, probably only large-group activities will be presented. Correlation of small-group or individual work becomes more difficult. This part of the program then needs to be in the hands of the other member of the team, the classroom teacher.

The music specialist may only have time to serve as consultant to the kindergarten program. In this case, time should be allowed each week for the two teachers to plan together. When serving as a resource person, the music specialist should do more than find songs or recordings. Contributions should include assistance in planning and in gathering manipulative objects and musical instruments for sound studies.

Summary

An environment for learning comprises space, people, objects, and time for exploration. The environment should pique the child's curiosity by creating an atmosphere of inquiry. It can be very sophisticated or simple, teacher-devised or commercially prepared. The learning environment is highly individualized for Threes and Fours with more group interaction opportunities for Fives. Many of the activities and learning environments described for the preschool child are appropriate for the kindergartener, too. If the kindergartener has not encountered some of the activities, they can be viewed as introductory explorations. This older child will deal with the ideas at a much faster rate but will still find them meaningful.

Sound control within a music environment is not really possible without great expense. The child is not so distracted by the layers of sound as is the teacher. As the child is usually distracted more by a visual than by an auditory stimulus, screens and other specially designed areas help focus the child's attention on the material at hand.

The Child and Movement 3

Look at me! Look at me!

I'm a frog under a tree.

Look at me! Look at me!

I'm a fish in the sea.

Look at me! Look at me!

I'm a little boy—just turned three.

Cries of "Look at me!" are frequently heard as children move excitedly through their day. This is the best advice an adult could receive, for the child's conscious and subconscious movements tell us many things. The child understands much that he cannot yet put into words. He is able, however, to demonstrate these understandings through gestures and other movements. Through careful observation, we can gain some insight into what the child is thinking.

Movement thus becomes an important nonverbal tool for learning. Evaluation as to the extent of learning is immediately possible: How descriptive are the child's movement responses to sounds that are long or short, high or low, fast or slow, of contrasting timbre? These contrasting ideas represent concepts at the core of understanding how sounds are organized into music. Many basic music concepts can be introduced through movement.

When children are first involved in movement, the experience should be as unstructured as possible. Such a typical activity as moving to the basic beat (marching around the room to music) is considered to be a structured response, for a marching response demands accurate stepping at a precise time. Some young children are able to march but not all of them will do so to the **same** beat.

A less structured response would be one motivated through words or imagery:

Can you open and close with this sound? Or this?

When observing the less structured experience, the teacher notes the difference in the nature and quality of the child's movement. The child is more apt to find success in an expressive movement of this kind, since there is no one "right" way to respond.

Learning through movement may occur in a developmental sequence beginning with expressive movement and evolving logically into more patterned responses. Through this approach, children gain two learning tools:

1. The use of movement to acquire musical understandings;
2. A growing repertoire of movement ideas.

Girls and boys should have many opportunities to respond with abandon to the totality of music. A variety of selections that elicit such movements as swaying, swinging, or thrusting should be presented. Children should also be able to express specific sound ideas that are played individually or heard as a prominent part of a musical selection.

Expressive Movement

The child's initial movements are centered on his own body. The three-year-old is still labeling and identifying objects and is not always ready to **be** something else. To "be a butterfly" presupposes knowledge of what a butterfly is and how it moves. The Three may or may not be ready for this experience.

The following suggestions demonstrate a developmental sequence with expressive movement evolving into patterned activities. **These suggestions are to be used as examples.** The teacher will need to create additional ones for each level of development if children are to be provided with enough repetition for learning to take place. A list of resource materials will be found in the bibliography (page 193).

MOVEMENT CENTERED ON SELF _____

1. **Teacher sits on the carpet, playing on a tambourine sounds that motivate or reinforce movement responses.**

Can you make your head dance? Fingers? Shoulder?

All of you?
Can you walk? Make your walk special? Silly? Funny?

Teacher taps the tambourine each time the child's foot touches the floor. Depending on the child's movement, the walking pattern may be uneven or even.

2. Play a **sound and silence** game by making up a musical version of the outdoor game *Red Rover*. Three or four children begin at the fence. When each name is called, the child moves with the sound and freezes (stands still) when the sound stops.

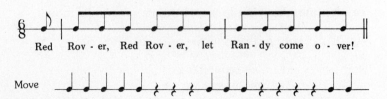

Red Rov - er, Red Rov - er, let Ran - dy come o - ver!

Move

When Randy reaches teacher, a quick hug is offered; then the next child is called. The Three will want to repeat this game endlessly.

3. Move in special ways to *sound and silence*. The teacher chants and plays on the maracas:

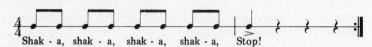

Shak - a, shak - a, shak - a, shak - a, Stop!

Repeat the pattern several times.

Another time, repeat the game in this manner:

Find the funniest way to stop!

Another funny way . . .

another . . .

How many ways can you move with this "shak-a" sound?

4. Respond to a particular *quality of sound,* like the clicking, staccato sounds produced by wood. Use a "Jumping Jack," an Appalachian rhythm toy sometimes called a Lumber Jack (available upon request at many music stores). Introduce "Mr. Jumping Jack." Allow time for exploration; then continue:

Can you make Jack dance?

The children hold Jack while teacher taps the board to make the feet clatter. Later, they trade jobs.

Can you dance with Mr. Jumping Jack?

Teacher uses Jumping Jack and chants while child moves.

> Clitter, clatter,
> What's the matter?
> Make your feet go
> Spicker-spatter!
> A-spic, a-spat, a-spic, a-spat!
> Now what do you think of that?

Play the game several times, using different parts of the body instead of feet—fingers, toes, eyelids "go spicker-spatter!"

5. Move to **sustained sounds**. A sustained sound often motivates smooth, legato movements. The young child has probably not explored this kind of movement as much as the more active responses. Use the following idea to help develop a feeling for this kind of response.

Distribute small paper cups to each child, and pour a half-inch of water into each as the child holds it.

Can you carry your cup of water carefully so that you will not bump into a friend? Teacher plays recorder or hums a legato melody as children move. *Can you carry your cup high? Low? Middle? Drink your water. Can you pretend the water is still there and move again?* Repeat the musical accompaniment. *Place your cup on the floor. Can you move as you did when the cup was in your hand?* Again, repeat music. Play music that expresses a smooth, legato idea, perhaps "Nocturne" from *Divertissement* by Ilbert or "The Swan" from *Carnival of the Animals* by Saint-Saëns.

6. Respond to *long and short sounds*. The teacher chants, then plays contrasting sound ideas. Children move, expressing their response to sounds. The chant alternates with each set of sounds.

> Listen to the sounds!
> They'll tell you how to move,
> Sometimes ziggy—
> And sometimes smooth.

Maracas

short, accented sounds
   (tap in palm of hand)

continuous smooth sound
   (roll seeds around by holding maraca upside down)

Piano

short staccato sounds

sustained sounds with hold
   pedal down

Drum

short sounds by thumping

long sounds by rubbing head
   of drum

Children soon develop names and concepts of things, enabling them to use imagery. Now delightful "let's pretend" ideas can elicit movement experiences.

1. *Have you ever seen a straight stick?*

Are there any straight sticks in our room? Children may point to small flagpole, pointer, or popsicle sticks.

Can you make a straight stick with your arm?

Teacher uses drum to accompany movement by playing single accented beat.

Can you make a straight stick with the other arm? *With one leg?*

Can you make one straight stick with two arms?

2. *Is this a straight stick?*

No, it's a bent stick.
Can you make a crooked stick with one arm?
Two arms?   *One leg?*

With two arms and two legs?

3. *Slowly make a round curved line with one arm.* Teacher uses finger cymbals to initiate movement. Encourage children to use all of the sound to form the curved line, then "freeze . . . unfreeze"!
Slowly make a big round ball with two arms.

4. *Combine curved and straight movements.* Rhythmically speak the chant.

> Circle around, circle around
> Up the pole, down to the ground.

What small part of your body could you move as you say the chant? Nose? Toes? Tongue? Eyes? Later repeat the chant. *This time you may not use words to say the chant . . . only sounds.* Invite one child to choose an instrument that has several pitches. *How can you "say" this chant on the xylophone?*

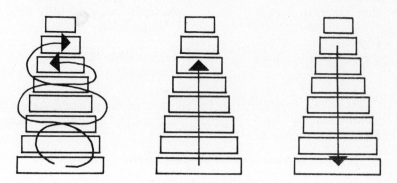

Circle around, circle around.

Up the pole, down to the ground!

Children should have much freedom when musically expressing this chant on the xylophone; however, "up" should be a high sound, "down" a low sound.

Perform the chant several times while moving parts of the body in sequence. Begin with smaller movement and end with a larger, as in a progression of fingers, arm, and then total body.

5. *Can you be a crayon?* Teacher uses a tambourine for sounds.

What color are you?

Are you a brand-new or an old crayon?

Can you color a beautiful picture?

Can you color a scribbly picture?

Can you be a crayon that falls off the table and breaks?

Can you be a crayon that was left in the summer sun at noon?

ff   *p*

6. Can you be a marshmallow? Teacher uses sandpaper blocks for sounds.

If you are a stiff marshmallow, show me!

If you are a soft marshmallow, show me!

If you were dropped, would you bounce or break?

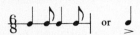 or

What would happen if you were toasted on a stick over a fire?

After being toasted, if you were dropped would you be stiff? Sticky? Runny?

7. What can you think of that opens and closes? The children may suggest flowers, doors, mouth.

Open and close to short and long sounds. Teacher uses words like "in" and "close," "out" and "open." Provide many opportunities to use these movements in contrasting responses to different qualities of sounds.

How many different ways can you open and close as the

sounds are played? Teacher uses different sounds of instruments. *All of you!* (Slowly open and close.)

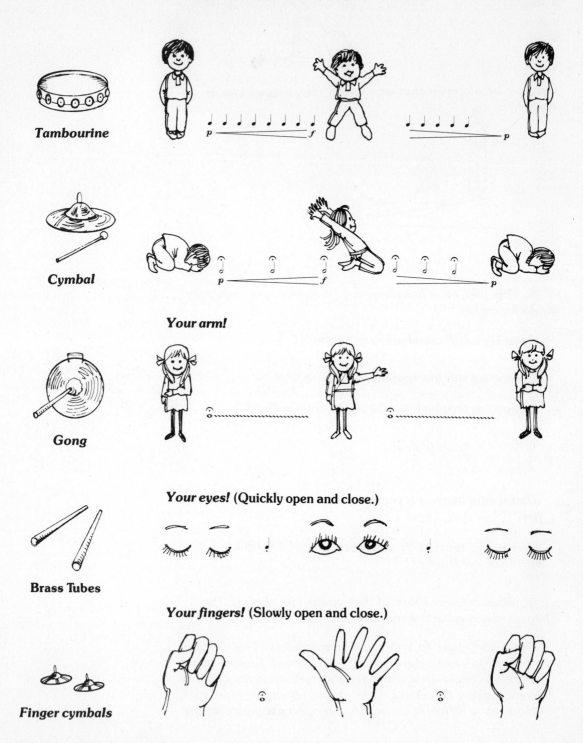

Tambourine

Cymbal

Your arm!

Gong

Your eyes! (Quickly open and close.)

Brass Tubes

Your fingers! (Slowly open and close.)

Finger cymbals

The teacher will need to notice the differences in movement quality as it relates to specific sounds. Did the children use short, jagged or long, sustained movements appropriate to sounds played?

8. *This is my stick.* Distribute short bamboo garden sticks to the children. Alternate singing the song with demonstrating the many ways to make the stick move. Accompany movements with the hand drum.

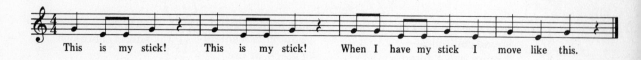

This is my stick! This is my stick! When I have my stick I move like this.

How many different ways can you walk with your stick?

This stick is magic. It can become anything you want it to be.

This is my "mous-tache" ... (all echo)   When I have a "mous-tache" I move like this.
(child says)

Point to one child, who fills in word telling what the stick will be. The child then demonstrates the idea: "This is my mustache . . . or hairbow, or snake!"

9. Use *sequence* in movement to tell a story.

I see a butterfly, sound asleep. Its wings are closed—they don't even flutter! A bell softly rings—the wings slowly begin to open.

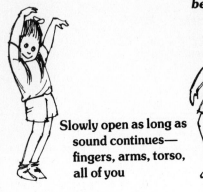

Slowly open as long as sound continues— fingers, arms, torso, all of you

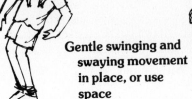

Gentle swinging and swaying movement in place, or use space

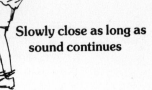

Slowly close as long as sound continues

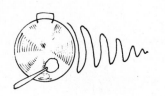

Gong or large cymbal

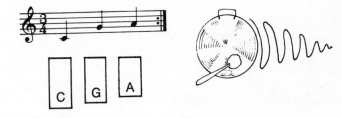

Did you think to move high, low, behind, to the side?

10. *Swing and sway.* Play a repeated accompaniment pattern on the xylophone or piano.

Sing a three-tone chant as children improvise a swinging or swaying movement.

Saturday's Children

1. Sat - ur - day's child - ren swing and sway.   Hey! Hey!   An - y old way.
2. Sun - day's child - ren... (Use all days of the week) ...

Can you swing high?   Can you swing low?   Round and round   A - way you go.

Ask a child or another adult to play the accompaniment while the teacher adds an improvised melodic interlude between verses. Use recorder, piano, or another xylophone. The pitches for improvisation may be C D E G A. Children continue moving during the interlude.

Use recorded selections that move with a feeling of three beats to the measure like "Let's Go Fly A Kite" from *Mary Poppins*.

Girls and boys should continue to use expressive movement throughout their school experiences. They are thus provided with opportunities to explore the many ways they can move through space, interacting with objects and other people. In the process, they will make valuable judgments and test their own decisions.

Inherent in much music of the Western world is the feeling of an underlying beat. A child cannot be involved with music of our culture for very long without becoming aware of this pulse. His body begins to respond to the feeling of pulse and of how other sounds relate to this steady beat. Some children respond quickly and with great accuracy while others, often because of auditory or coordination problems, are less able to do so.

When guiding children from expressive movement to more structured responses, the teacher should use transitional activities. One begins where the child is, matching the individual's movements, gradually drawing him to the beat and tempos established by the music.

1. *Matching the child's beat.* Teacher accompanies movement using hand drum.

Do you have a house? Is it a big house or a little house?

Show me the floor of your house.

Does your house have walls?

If they are rough, show me!

If they are smooth, show me!

Does your house have a ceiling? If it is rough, show me!

Continue playing appropriate sounds on the drum as children respond to statements and questions. *If it is smooth, show me!*
Does your house have windows?
Does your house have a door? A door knob?
Open the door. Step outside and close the door with a big slam.

Transition to Patterned Movement

Swishing sound on drum head

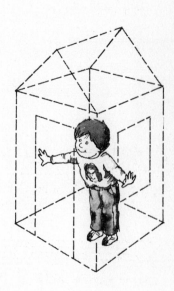

Rodney, show me how you can walk around the outside of your house. Susy, show me how you can walk. . . .

Provide several opportunities for individuals to walk around their houses. Use the hand drum and play sounds each time the child's feet touch the ground. The sounds may be slow, fast, even, or uneven, depending on how the child is moving. The teacher follows the child and does not impose a tempo upon the child's movement.

Play this game many times, varying where the child may walk, perhaps to visit a neighbor or to a store or shopping center. After children have had time to associate the sound of the drum with moving feet, change the game so that the children begin to follow the sounds of the drum. Choose a child who is moving with a fairly accurate steady beat and whose tempo is just about right for the short-legged stride of the other children.

Susy walks around her house in such a nice way. Let's all walk around our house just like Susy. Open your door. Are you ready to go? Teacher plays Susy's steady beat while all children try to match the sound.

2. **Stick game.** Place bamboo garden sticks on the floor. Use walking, running, hopping movements to go over the sticks. (Bamboo sticks are especially useful since they do not roll readily under the feet of the child nor break so easily as wooden dowels.)

The teacher plays the drum each time the child's feet touch the ground.

Can you step over the sticks?
What funny way can you step over the sticks?
Who has another funny way?
Can you hop over the sticks? Jump? Go sideways? Backwards?
Can you go over the sticks quickly? Very slowly?
Can you go over the sticks in the smoothest way possible?
The "jiggiest" way possible?
Who can follow the drum and go over the sticks this way?

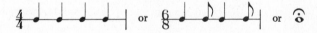

3. Find many ways to play these *follow-the-sound* games by varying them topically. Alternate the following chants with movement.

Linnet, linnet,
Come this minute.
Here's a house with something in it.
How will you come? Let me see?
One! Two! Three!

One child moves as teacher matches the child's beat using hand drum or recorder. Later the teacher plays and the child matches teacher's sounds.

> Open the gates to the castle moat.
> Here comes the king (queen) in a white fur coat.

Two children form a gate with hands. One by one the children "assume royalty" and pass under the gate. Teacher follows their movement with sounds of hand drum or recorder. Later, children follow teacher's sounds.

> Dibble dee dee, dibble dee dop,
> Look at me! I can hop!

Child improvises own hop. Teacher matches child's movement with sound of woodblock.
   Another time, vary the chant:

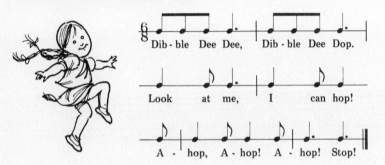

Dib - ble Dee Dee, Dib - ble Dee Dop.

Look   at me,   I   can hop!

A - hop, A - hop! A - hop! Stop!

In this version, the child follows the rhythm pattern of the words.

   4. Do as I do. Provide experiences where children grow in ability to follow movements as closely as possible. Again, move from the less demanding to the more accurate response.
   Hold a mirror in front of individual children.

Can you make a movement that you can see in the mirror? Was the movement in the mirror the same as yours? Let's pretend I am looking in a mirror and you are my reflection. Can you move exactly as I do?

   Teacher slowly moves one arm in various ways. Children follow, performing at the same time. If the teacher uses left arm, children should use the right arm so that the movement is an exact mirror.
   The teacher may bend low, reach high, curl finger in and out. All movements are very slow so that they are easy to follow. Later, use two arms or the whole body.

Add sounds or a musical selection to accompany the activity. The music should reflect the sustained quality of the movement:

- strum strings of piano while depressing the hold pedal
- strum strings of Autoharp with no chord bars down
- play random sounds on metallophone
- play such recorded selections as *Syrinx* by Debussy (a legato flute solo that works well for movements using sustained quality)

Responding to the Underlying Beat

1. Sing and move as I do. Songs like *Clap Your Hands* are excellent for teaching response to the basic beat because the first words of the song tell the child exactly what and when to move:

"Clap,   clap,   clap your . . .

Clap Your Hands

Interlude

3. Nod, nod, nod your head,
Nod your heads together,
Nod, nod, nod your head,
Nod your heads together.

4. Shake, shake, shake your head,
Shake your heads together,
Shake, shake, shake your head,
Shake your heads together.

5. Stretch, stretch, stretch up high,
Stretch up high together,
Stretch, stretch, stretch up high,
Stretch up high together.

6. Dig, dig, dig the ground,
Dig the ground together,
Dig, dig, dig the ground,
Dig the ground together.

7. Crawl, crawl, crawl along,
Crawl along together,
Crawl, crawl, crawl along,
Crawl along together.

2. Step with sounds or after sounds.
Can you step on raindrops? Step when you hear the sounds. Teacher plays finger cymbals or triangle.

Can you step on the raindrops after you hear the sounds?

Can you carry a ball? Gather up a great big beach ball in your arms. After each step, bump the bottom of the beach ball with your knee. Move when you hear the sounds.

Step   Bump   Step   Bump

Use a larger cymbal. Play the half-note pattern. The "bump" action is to establish a feeling of the underlying second and fourth beat, making it easier for the child to step the pattern more accurately. Repeat the activity by having children move after hearing the sound.

Movement should not be limited to responding to sounds of one instrument or word image. If an association is to be made that the beat underlies music, then music must be used. Recorded selections, singing games, piano accompaniments, and other instrumental ensembles are a vital part of teaching movement to music. There are many sources of these materials. Those found in the Kindergarten Basic Music texts have been carefully screened for use. The following singing games, piano selections, and suggested recordings are representative of these resources. Further material is listed in the bibliography (page 193).

A SINGING GAME

Shake That Little Foot, Dinah-O

Rhythmically   Folk Song from Texas / Arranged by Rosemary Jacques.

1. Old Aunt Di - nah went to town   Rid - ing a bil - ly goat, lead - ing a hound,
2. Hound dog barked and billy goat jumped,   Set Aunt_ Di - nah straddle of a stump,

*Most children will "shake that little foot" at first. Encourage imaginative movement, like rocking from one foot to the other, shrugging the shoulder, bending from side to side.

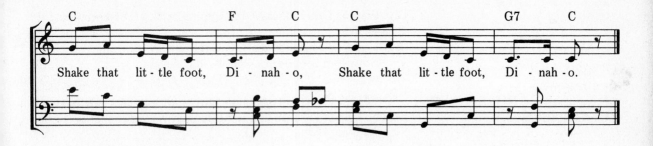

Shake that lit-tle foot, Di - nah -o, Shake that lit-tle foot, Di - nah -o.

3. Sift the meal and save the bran,
   Give it to the old cow to make her stand, . . .

4. Old Aunt Dinah sick in bed,
   Sent for the doctor, the doctor said, . . .

5. Get up, Dinah, you ain't sick,
   All you need is a hickory stick, . . .

6. I like sugar in my coffee-o,
   Some folks they won't have it, no, . . .

Children will probably respond to this music by making sharp, thrusting, quick, short movements. When playing this as an accompaniment for movement, be sure to contrast the first accented beat with others in the measure.

How will you move to sounds that are louder? Softer?

For Children, Vol. 1, No. XXXII

Fast

Béla Bartók

There are many recorded selections of music that moves with a strong underlying beat. Among them are the following:

"In the Hall of the Mountain King" from *Peer Gynt Suite* by E. Grieg

"One Foot, Other Foot" from *Allegro* by R. Rodgers

"**Step in Time**" from *Mary Poppins* **by R. M. Sherman and R. B. Sherman**

"**Children's March**" **by R. F. Goldman**

"**Stars and Stripes Forever**" **by J. P. Sousa**

Movement in Relation to the Underlying Beat

After having moved with the basic underlying beat, girls and boys may be helped to sense that some sounds may be longer or shorter than the basic beat.

1. **Perform chants *in relation to the underlying beat.*** Establish the beat:

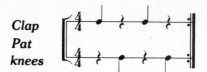

Chant

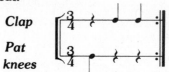

My name is (Bet-ty) and I want to (play).
My name is (Ev-an) and I want to (sleep).

Establish this beat:

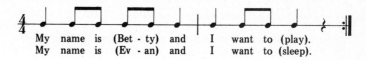

Chant

Bil-ly, Wil-ly, Nil-ly, Some-one said you're sil-ly, Show me! Show me!

Billy makes up a silly movement while others continue to clap the beat. Change name to next child by saying, "Suzy, Silly, Nilly" or "Janie, Jillie, Nilly."

2. **Ask a child or another adult to play an underlying beat on either of the following instruments:**

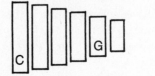

Rhythmically chant

Hal - ley hal - ley has - tle   Come in - to my cas - tle   This is the way to   come.—

Children move one at a time to the "castle." Teacher uses pitches C D E G A and plays with the beat or twice or four times as long. The child follows what the teacher is playing:

Teacher plays

First child steps

Teacher plays

Second child steps

3. Use the *shortest sounds in the rhythm pattern* for the underlying pulse. In much of today's popular music, the shortest sound is used for the underlying beat. Create many accompaniments using this approach.

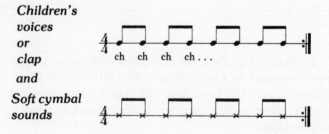

Children's voices or clap

ch   ch   ch   ch . . .

and

Soft cymbal sounds

Teacher dictates patterns for children to echo while they are maintaining the sound of the shortest sound with voices or claps.

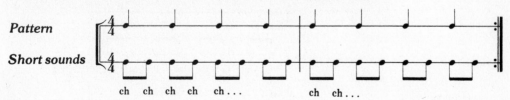

Pattern

Short sounds

ch ch ch ch   ch . . .   ch ch . . .

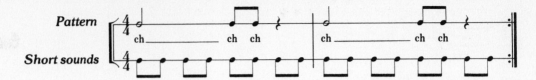

By approaching echo clapping from the short-sound accompaniment, it is possible to dictate slightly more complicated patterns, such as:

Use this idea of the short-sound accompaniment with this song. (The shortest sound in the song is ♪ .)

Sing while tapping or playing the shortest sound on the cymbal. Clap the rhythm pattern of the words with the sound of the cymbal.

A B C

Traditional Melody
Words from Mother Goose

Key: C Starting Tone: C (1)

A, B, C,   Tum-ble down D,   The cat's in the cup-board and   can't see me.

4. Echo Clap. Children need to have experiences using small motor muscles in clapping precise patterns. Through this involvement they will learn how one sound relates to another. The teacher claps a short pattern while chanting word syllables; children echo.

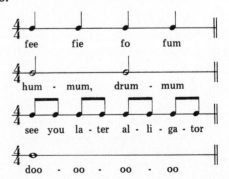

Combine these long and short sounds to create rhythm patterns:

hum   mum   fee   fie

Echo clap patterns in relation to the underlying beat. Ask one child to play the beat or shorter sound while you dictate patterns to be echoed by the class.

5. *Rhythm patterns of the words.* The rhythm pattern of the words is made up of sounds that are the same as or longer or shorter than the basic beat. Sing songs while responding to basic beat, clap rhythm patterns of the words, and combine ideas using two body movements.

London Bridge

Traditional Song Game

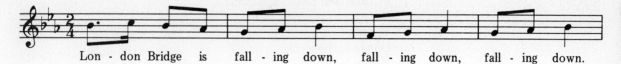

Lon - don Bridge is fall - ing down, fall - ing down, fall - ing down.

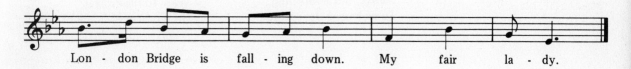

Lon - don Bridge is fall - ing down. My fair la - dy.

First time

Sing and walk with the basic beat.

Second time

Sing and clap the rhythm pattern of the words.

etc.

Third time

Do both at the same time.

Fourth time

> *Take the words inside; move your lips but do not sing. Now, try to walk the beat and clap the rhythm pattern of the words.*

Dance

Dance is a conscious activity requiring an accurate rhythmic response. When one *recreates* a dance, it is predetermined that there will be

1. a certain space used;
2. structure involved;
3. performance of the dance.

Dance uses floor patterns and gestures that involve repetition and contrast. These movements may be planned for short ideas, longer phrases, or large sections of the music. The music may come about as a result of the dance, or the dance may be planned to follow the music.

Many simple and appropriate dance materials exist for the use of young children. Such materials as "play party" games and circle, folk, and novelty dances are included in most kindergarten basic music texts. The following examples are typical of those used at this level.

A very simple dance is performed as children sing the song.
Formation: Stand in a circle.

Words	**Movement**
Dance in the circle,	Walk to the right,
Dance in the ring,	Walk to the left,
Dance in the morning,	Walk to the center,
To welcome the spring.	Step backwards out of circle.

Dance in the Circle (6-7)

Key: C / Starting Tone: C (1)
Meter:

Louisiana French Folk Song

Dance in the cir - cle, dance in the ring;

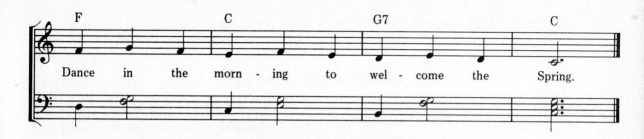

Invite children to perform this circle dance. They will need to stand in a circle and move to the following floor pattern while singing the song.

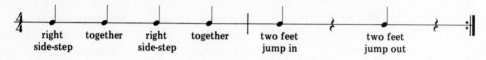

| right side-step | together | right side-step | together | two feet jump in | | two feet jump out | |

I Went to the River

Freely improvised call

Setting by B.A.

I went to the ri - ver, ri - ver, ri - ver.

2. I couldn't get across, cross, cross.

3. I paid five dollars, dollars, dollars.

4. For an old gray hoss, hoss, hoss.

5. That hoss wouldn't pull, pull, pull.

6. So I swapped him for a bull, bull, bull.

7. And the bull wouldn't holler, holler, holler.

8. So I swapped him for a dollar, dollar, dollar.

9. And the dollar wouldn't spend, spend, spend.

10. So I put it in the grass, grass, grass.

11. And the grass wouldn't grow, grow, grow.

12. So I gets myself a hoe, hoe, hoe.

13. And the hoe wouldn't chop, chop, chop.

14. So I took it to the shop, shop, shop.

15. And the shop took my money, money, money.

16. So goodbye my honey, honey, honey.

17. Well, that's all chu chu chu, chu, chu.

18. Well, that's all. . . .

xylophone or violin accompaniment

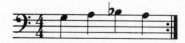

A Synthesis Experience

The child should have opportunity to use the many movement ideas acquired to improvise in a more sophisticated manner.

CREATE A SPACE SAGA

Ask for the children's suggestions on various movement and musical ways to express ideas about a space story.

Typical suggestions might be these:

Story Sequence	Movement	Music
10 – 9 – 8 – 7 – 6 – 5 – 4 – 3 – 2 – 1	begin low; open; spiral up; spin; turn	loud percussion sounds; upward glissando on xylophone or piano
*Walk in space	use slow controlled movements; balance; sustained; smooth	strum piano strings while holding sustain pedal down
Return to Earth	slow spiral downward	downward glissando on xylophone or piano
Splash down	very low; swaying with waves	loud percussion sounds; play a meter pattern on metallophone, bells, or piano

Summary

Girls and boys use movement with music both to satisfy the urge to explore how their bodies can move through space and to communicate innermost feelings about the music they are hearing. Movement to music, while foremost an esthetic experience, is also a most practical and efficient means of teaching children basic information about music. Understandings covered in a developmental sequence provide a core through which one may be certain that entry behaviors for future learning have been established. A strict reliance

*It is great fun to close curtains, then flick the light switch quickly on and off for a strobe light effect during this part. Make children aware of this, since it may visually disorient the performer, frightening the unprepared child.

on sequence to such extent that one does not repeat previous levels would be a grave mistake. Expressive movement has been described as a place to begin, but there should be no closure on this type of experience. Upper-grade youngsters should continue to express themselves and to acquire further information through the freedom of this approach.

The developmental sequence projected for movement in early childhood is this:

- **Expressive Movement Centered on Self**

  How many ways can the child move to long and short; high and low; fast and slow; smooth and jagged; loud and soft; various timbres of sound?

- **Imagery in Movement**

  Children respond to sounds and music through such movement as thrusting, swinging, swaying, opening and closing, short and sharp, and multidirectional levels. Children deal with sequence through movement.

- **Transition to Patterned Movement**

  Teacher responds to the child's beat. The child then grows in ability to respond to the beat of others.

- **Responding to the Underlying Beat**

  Children move with sounded beat, with beat "internalized."

- **Movement in Relation to the Underlying Beat**

  Children become aware of longer and shorter sounds in relation to the beat. These longer and shorter sounds are combined to form rhythm patterns. Children also move to the rhythm pattern of the words.

- **Dance**

  Children learn to make specific use of space and to work within a structure.

The approach to movement in early childhood is process-oriented, based on the child's ability to respond at a given level of physical development. Association with musical sounds begins by utilizing both the more predictable responses to a single, uncluttered sound source and the free response to the totality of a musical selection.

The Child And Singing 4

Squeal, Cry,

Gurgle, Coo!

Can't you hear?
I'm talking to you!

Children use their voices from the day they are born. At first, their sounds signal needs to those around them. As these sounds are reinforced, babies learn to use them in meaningful ways; a cry signals discomfort, a coo, pleasure. While functionally using sounds, children also explore the many ways to manipulate them, taking great delight in their product. This playful approach allows them to discover high-low, long-short, and loud-soft contrasts as well as the many vocal timbres of bubbling, growling, hissing, and the like. These various sounds represent the basic elements of music and are thus the beginnings of songmaking.

When dealing with the vocal development of the very young child, we have traditionally used the technique of songmaking through imitation. We have composed songs that require simple to complex rhythm, melodic, and language responses. We have depended on repetition, assuming that if the song is repeated many times, the child will eventually perform it well. We have burdened the child with the "structured−composed" song, conveying the message that there is one and only one way to perform even a simple melody. On the other hand, we have given little consideration to the child's own world of music, which is rich in improvisation and does not require a preset response.

The structured song approach has succeeded insofar as we have in many instances wisely used children's folk literature that has been passed down from generation to generation. This literature has survived because children through the ages have felt it to be right, but with the more structured approach to singing, children often labor long to perform even simple folk material. They finally find varying degrees of performance success in the late fourth or fifth year. This leaves the song world of the Threes and early Fours at a stage where a single focus on the structured song may not be the most appropriate.

Isolating three- and four-year-olds from composed (structured) songs is neither possible nor desirable. Children's performance of structured songs, however, can be coupled with more attention to their own improvisations, thus creating a program that better meets their needs.

Guiding the Learning Process

The opportunity to work with the child as an individual is greater during the preschool years than at any other time in the educational process; guidance is given by parents, teachers, other adults, and children. With understanding of the child and the learning process, adults can help girls and boys grow in skills both as creators of songs and as performers of the music of others. A sequential program that develops skills, understandings, and a creative posture toward songmaking is presented in the following material.

The Parents' Role

People in the home reinforce the young child's use of vocal sounds in many ways. Parents can share many lovely melodies with baby from the very beginning. Parents should be provided, through meetings and newsletters, with information and encouragement to make music with their children. Most parents are eager to be a part of the child's early music education and need only a few suggestions to initiate useful experiences.

It is important that both father and mother participate in musical moments. Songs or rhythmic games may be traditional or spontaneously made up. Times and places for music-making abound:

1. Rock baby while singing lullabies.
2. Sing and rhythmically rub powder on baby's stomach after bathing.
3. Sing nonsense sounds at bath time while water is dribbling on baby's back or he is "feeling" the squeeze of the wet washcloth or sponge toy.
4. Rhythmically tap baby's feet together after changing diaper.
5. Make in-and-out motions with arms as a part of song games.
6. Provide a place in the kitchen for the crawler to reach empty

cans, old pans, wooden spoons for banging. Occasionally add "bling-blang" melody to baby's sounds.

Bling - Blang

7. Place beans inside a clean plastic detergent bottle with securely sealed cap. Add this rattling sound to the kitchen sounds.

Musical Games

From the time the baby is two or three months old, parents can play sound games, imitating baby's gurgles and other vocal sounds. The game becomes "Who Is Copying Whom?" for either the baby makes the sound and the parent echoes or just the opposite occurs.

More sophisticated games can soon be played. Parents may rhythmically speak the following chants or add their own melody to them. Melodies using limited pitches are easily added to the rhythm of the chant:

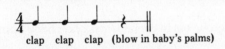

Parents should be encouraged to trust their own musical judgment in making up these simple tunes.

1. **Pease Porridge Hot**
   Move baby's hands while chanting or singing:

   clap clap clap (blow in baby's palms)

   Pease porridge hot *(blow),*
   Pease porridge cold *(blow),*
   Pease porridge in the pot
   Nine days old *(blow).*

2. **Nose Blower**
   Touch the named part of baby's body while chanting or singing:

   Nose blower,
   Eye blinker,
   Mouth eater,
   Chin chopper *(tickle chin)!*

Here is a more complicated variation of the same game:

Brow bender,
Eye peeper,
Nose dropper,
Mouth eater,
Chin chopper!
Knock at the door *(tap forehead),*
Ring the bell, *(push on stomach),*
Lift up the latch *(raise nose),*
Walk in *(put finger in mouth).*
Take a chair.

3. One, Two, Three

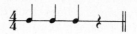

One, two, three *(walk fingers from toes to knees),*
Tickle your knee.
Four, five, six *(fingers continue to stomach),*
Pick up sticks.
Seven, eight, nine *(fingers continue to chin),*
You're all mine *(hug).*

4. Pat-a-Cake

Pat-a-cake, pat-a-cake, baker's man *(pat hands together),*
Roll 'em out, roll 'em out fast as you can *(roll hands),*
Pat 'em and punch 'em *(clap hands together, touch palms with finger)*
And throw 'em in the pan *(toss open baby's arms).*

5. Rub-a-Dub-Dub

Rub-a-dub-dub *(rub baby's stomach),*
Three men in a tub.
How do you think they got there?
They wiggled and sniggled *(fingers mysteriously walk on stomach),*
And moved very close,
Then jumped up into the air *(make gentle swaying movements with baby in arms).*

6. Rub a Tummy

Rub a tummy,
Touch a toe,
Three little pigs,
Said, "Oh! Oh! Oh!" *(Pull different toe on each "oh.")*

7. See-saw, Margery Daw
Touch baby's toes while playing this game.

> See-saw, Margery Daw,
> The old hen flew over the malt house.
> She counted her chickens one by one,
> Still she missed the little white one,
> And this is it, this is it, this is it! *(Pull little toe.)*

8. This Little Pig Went to Market
Begin by touching big toe, moving to each toe in turn.

> This little pig went to market;
> This little pig stayed home;
> This little pig had roast beef;
> This little pig had none;
> This little pig went "week! week! week!"
> All the way home.

9. Nose Fun

> My mother and your mother
> Went over the way;
> Said my mother to your mother,
> "It's chop-a-nose day." *(Gently pull nose.)*

10. Shoe a Little Horse
Pat the soles of baby's feet while chanting or singing:

> Shoe a little horse,
> Shoe a little mare,
> But let the colt go
> Bare, bare, bare.

11. Bibble-dee Bobble-dee Boo
Play a hide-and-seek game.

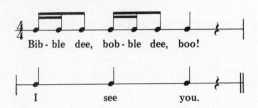

12. Whistle Play
Whistle a tune while holding baby. Baby will undoubtedly put finger to your lips, stopping the sound. Play a musical stop-and-start game with much "let's pretend" commotion when baby stops the whistle.

Many songs to sing for baby, including lullabies and nursery rhymes, may be chosen from the wide collection found in children's literature. When singing, if it seems appropriate, clap hands or dance for or with baby. Many joyful times come about by incorporating spontaneous musical play into the infant's day.

Recorded Vocal Music

Vocal music in the home is also provided by television, radio, and record players. Television features much music in programs especially planned for children, music usually in the form of clever and appealing pop tunes. The preschool child tends to use this music for what we will label a secondary purpose. The music serves as an instructional tool for learning letters and words, socializing skills, and self-concepts. Although the music is generally far too difficult for children to sing accurately, they are fully capable of hearing and enjoying it. They should not be pressured to reproduce these songs accurately, but should simply be allowed to decide what of each song they wish to use.

Girls and boys will begin early to build their own values regarding the use of songs. As a part of setting the conditions that foster values, they must have an opportunity to hear a wide variety of music representing various cultures and styles. Children are not locked into Western tonalities or any given style; thus, carefully selected songs from operas or Oriental culture would be quite appropriate as a part of the nursery listening repertoire.

A typical recorded song album for children is performed by one artist; thus, there are a dozen or more melodies all by the same voice. Because children love repetition, the dozen melodies could be enough to hold their interest for an extended period of time. Rather than confining listening to just one voice, however, a collection of several artists representing voices of men, women, and children solo, in small vocal ensembles, or in large choirs should be used.

Many of the most noted composers grew up in a musically enriched home environment. From their earliest years, music was a significant part of their family lives. Further, they received parental approval of their first musical efforts. It is not our intent to produce a composer per family, but we believe that when a given value is modeled by those most loved and respected, the child, too, tends to hold it dear.

Functions of Preschool Singing

The **primary** function of preschool singing is to help children grow in these abilities:

1. To interact esthetically with vocal music;
2. To use voices in an expressive way;
3. To sing melodies created by self and others.

A **secondary** function of singing is to help children learn about themselves and their relation to the world by using songs that express values and ideas. When dealing with material from a topical standpoint, the teacher may choose a specific song, even though it is too difficult for children to sing musically accurately, because it includes important learning concepts for social growth or self-imagery. The teacher's goal for this experience is a more esthetic approach to teaching concepts other than music. The teacher does not necessarily expect or demand tone-matching. The child follows instructions given melodically, like "Point your finger in the air, to the floor, in front, behind. . . ."

When such a structured song is used with Threes and early Fours, the secondary behaviors, learning through music rather than focusing on music, tend to be reinforced and the effort to develop musical understandings is left in the domain of creative song play. As the child develops the auditory and physical skills to reproduce melodies more accurately, the primary and secondary functions of music begin to merge.

The teacher's ability to discern the difference between these two functions of songs will make possible more careful planning for the musical and total growth of children. The following observation is an example of a song experience in the preschool. Is it a primary or secondary experience?

Observing Children Learn

A group of young Fours scampered excitedly to the rug area. Teacher had just announced it was time to play a musical game. A recording was placed on the phonograph, and after a short introduction, a voice began to sing a clever song: "If you're wearing red, touch your nose. If you're wearing green, touch your toes." The teacher joined the recorded voice, sang the words, and modeled the actions. The children attempted to follow the instructions and imitate the movements of the teacher. As to singing the song, however, the participation was spotty, since only the most adept could listen, sing, and move simultaneously. Several children concentrated on following only the movement ideas. The children thoroughly enjoyed the experience and were eager to repeat it several times.

This activity is not classified as a primary song experience since it was beyond the children's ability to perform vocally. It is an activity of secondary musical function, for the children were learning to follow instructions and learning directions, body imagery, and color identification.

The terms **primary** and **secondary** do not mean that the secondary behaviors are less important. These terms are used only from the point of view of musical growth.

The Early Childhood Vocal Program

A plan for guiding the vocal needs of three- to five-year-old children should project a two-track approach that simultaneously uses the child's innate vocal musical ideas (own improvised songs) and the music of the culture (composed or folk vocal literature). Concerns for vocal development should include consideration for the child's range, ability to produce melodic and rhythmic patterns, tonal and rhythmic memory, and auditory discrimination skills.

Development of the child's own musical ideas may be approached in a variety of ways:

1. Playing with sounds (voice inflection games);
2. Creating through-composed melodies;
3. Echo singing;
4. Singing within a tonal center;
5. Creating songs that rhyme.

The ability to sing the structured songs of others requires the following skills:

1. Responding to rhythm in melody;
2. Matching tones of a melody;
3. Acquiring word and sequence memory.

The Child's Own Songs

Observed early behaviors of children squealing, crying, and laughing indicate that young voices have a wide range of pitch. When singing formally, however, girls and boys tend to stay within a limited range (d′−a′):

When first singing with or for another person, they may use a low, soft, chanting voice with only slight inflections; frequently, greater range and variation of pitch occur in improvised songs and sound-play games. The most usable singing pitches may consist of only two or three within the individual range possibilities. Initially, the child should be left in control of the range, for only he can make the decision of where it is most comfortable to sing.

Though a wider pitch range is possible for children, the early use of it is probably a matter of chance. Children do not consciously control specific highs and lows. Pitch variation is a result of the emotion of the game and posture of the body in action. Imitating the fire siren is an example of this tonal play.

Much use of sounds in play should be encouraged, for it provides opportunities for the voice to move freely, developing dexterity that will lead to later control of specific pitches.

The little singsong melodies that a child creates as a part of play are *through-composed* melodies. They have no definite rhythm or melodic organization; they are just wandering little tunes about toys, pets, or the child himself. The texts are as charming as the mind of the young performer, as logical only as is the child's thinking at that point. The song may begin, "My dolly has a pretty red dress," and end abruptly, "I'm hungry!" Through the singsong play episodes, the teacher can initiate singing conversations that often evolve into delightful operas with teacher and child each taking a role. With intermittent use of the echo play technique, this free musical play remains the central focus for vocal development of the three- and early-four-year-old.

More conscious effort is required to play even simple echo song games. Auditory discrimination and tonal and rhythmic memory underlie the response, and the child must focus on the complexities of hearing, imitating, and pitch control. As imitation is a major mode of learning for children this age, simple echo play games are greatly enjoyed.

Children eventually develop a self-satisfying need to sing with a feeling of tonal center. This feeling of tonality is not necessarily in the range established by another voice; the pitches are selected by the child. The tones of these improvised songs have a relationship to one another and show a degree of repetition. The songs may take the form of two-tone or three-tone chants and evolve out of play activities. The child is an avid creator of jingles and rhyming chants that become the lyrics of the song:

> Cinderella, dressed in yellow,
> Found a fellow made of jello!

Creating Songs

The child's own songs, are an important part of the vocal developmental process. These songs are freely improvised *(through-composed)*, used by the child at random. The adult can discreetly enter into the creative process yet leave the controls with the child. Intervention is possible within the daily play activities and occurs as a part of the language and movement games.

Singing is closely tied to language development. Language is acquired at a faster rate during the preschool years than at any other time. The pitch and dynamic contrasts resulting from the normal expressiveness of words become the natural materials for vocal improvisations. Words are easily turned into melodies.

VOICE INFLECTION GAMES _____

Begin by playing voice inflection games with children.

1. Copy Cat *Can you be a copy cat? Can you copy everything I say?*

Teacher

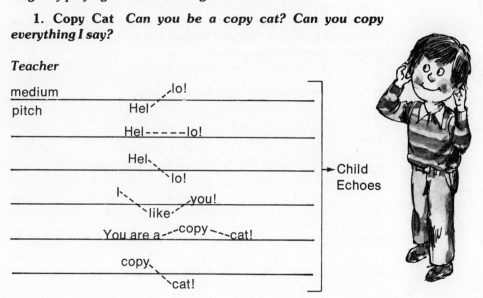

Teacher:

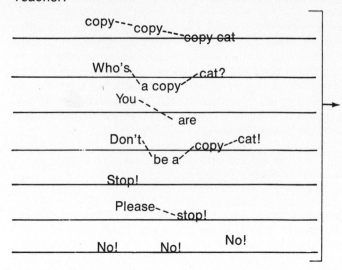

copy---copy---~~copy cat~~

Who's.   cat?
         \a copy/
You~
         ~ are

Don't.   copy---cat!
       \be a/

Stop!

Please--~stop!

No!   No!   No!

2. Puppet Song Play   The use of puppets in play often frees children to participate in an activity when the pressure of being themselves might be inhibiting. Younger children may manipulate finger puppets better than hand puppets. It is important that puppets represent people because mothers, fathers, policemen, brothers sing; animals do not. The association is thus enhanced that singing is an appropriate activity for children, since they, too, are "people."

Initially, puppet improvisations may be one-sided with teacher modeling most of the conversational song. The reluctant child can soon be coaxed to join the fun. To motivate participation, the teacher may begin with echo statements and then change to questions. This technique moves the child from pure imitation to creative responses.

Teacher (using voice inflection) Child answers

High   .lo
                    Hel-
Low

            Hi!

I.   ,you!
   ~like~

What's---~your~---~name?

Is----~your.   ,red?
          \dress/

Three-year-old Brian was playing in the music area. He poked his head out of the sound box. Teacher used "daddy" and "boy" puppets, singing conversationally. She invited Brian to take a puppet. Brian ignored the puppet but invited teacher to come into his house to play. Teacher accepted and, when inside, again offered a puppet to Brian, which he rejected a second time. Teacher began singing both roles. Brian did not sing but exhibited much careful listening as he played with other objects in the area. Three-year-old Amy entered the box. Brian became shy and soon left. Amy eagerly used the boy puppet in rapid conversation with teacher. Her sung responses were delightful and full of *her* music and imagination. Amy responded with great warmth and love to the puppets. "I like you, Daddy!" she sang, hugging the other puppet and at times making her puppet hug teacher, too.

A puppet singsong experience occurred between Julie and teacher.
Teacher (manipulating puppet)   "Hello, Julie!"
Julie (manipulating puppet, very softly answers with a mumbling response)   "Hello!"
Teacher   "I like you. Will you be my friend?"
Julie (softly)   "Yes."
Teacher   "I see your red dress."
  Julie does not answer, just examines red dress of puppet.
Teacher   "Where are your eyes?"
  Julie points to eyes of puppet.
Teacher   "Can you count the eyes?"
Julie (looks at puppet intently, points, and sings)   "One, two."
Teacher   "What color is this button?"
Julie (with pitch near that of teacher's question)   "Red."
Teacher (pointing to puppet)   "What color is this dress?"
Julie   "Red, and this is blue, and this is yellow. . . ."
  Julie abruptly, but happily, throws puppet down and runs to another activity.

3. Nonrestrictive Toys Nonrestrictive toys are most useful representations of singing people. These toys are figures with shape suggestive of the human form but not explicitly descriptive. The child may imagine them to be any characters that meet the play demands of the moment. They may be created from dowels the size of broomsticks. It is important that the figures have open mouths as though singing.

4. Now This game uses movement to motivate the use of varying voice inflections.

Form a circle in which girls and boys are seated. Ask one child to move within the middle of the ring. Each time this child's feet touch the ground, all the voices are to say the word "NOW."

Instructions for singing people
Cut a thin section of dowel for head. Drill two eyes and a larger mouth through this section. Attach head to round dowel body. Make figures different heights.

The game is played with different children taking turns moving. As the fun progresses, encourage children to respond to the movement of the dancer by speaking the word loudly if the individual steps with a heavy step, softly with a lighter step, high with tiptoe steps. The dancers soon discover that they can evoke many different sounds just by the manner in which they move. The dancer's body becomes the musical score for others to follow.

Through-composed Songs

Conversational song responses can be shaped into longer ideas. The complexity of the through-composed song is based on the child's increasing language skills. The high and low pitches of words become melodies. The eventual shape of the melody will flow from the length of the child's breath (phrase), the rise and fall of words (melody), and natural rhythm patterns of language (rhythm). The songs will initially have little balance in rhythm or phrase and few repeated patterns; by adult standards, they are rambling and loosely organized. Since these are such natural songs for children, the teacher will want to encourage their creation.

In order to do so, it is often necessary for the teacher to sing in this same through-composed style. The following are techniques for motivating these experiences.

1. Singsong Book Children observe adults reading books and soon imitate "reading." They huddle close to an adult, eagerly pointing to pictures, accurately and inaccurately naming things on the pages. The pages cannot be turned fast enough to satisfy the excitement of the game. The book may or may not be right side up throughout this activity.

This "reading" process lends itself perfectly to the motivation of through-composed melodies. Develop a book from which songs may be created. The pages may contain sketches or simple line drawings from which the child can easily perceive the story idea. Included on the page is music notation written on a staff. The notation merely signifies to the child that there is a different intent from the usual in this book. Neither child nor teacher is expected to follow the notation for melodic ideas. The notation merely signifies that this is a singing, not a reading book, as in the examples here.

a. *Sing about the chicken* First point to the whole egg. *"What's this?* Child needs little more motivation to sing a lovely song about chicken cracking the egg and saying, "Peep! peep!"

b. *Sing about the clown(s)*   Kathy made up a song that went on and on: "Once there was a clown and he did a trick. He standed on the ball with his finger, but he fell off, and broke his arm, and his leg, and his toe, and he hadda go to the doctor . . . and the doctor gave him a shot."

2. Bus Play   Occasionally enter into the children's play. Turn their conversations into song responses. Begin by singing questions.

Teacher entered into children's play using question techniques to motivate a singing response.

Observing Children Learn

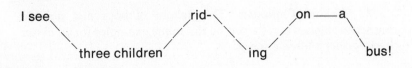

I see three children rid- ing on — a bus!

Children alternated between singing and speaking. Lucas chanted, "Spencer's in the front of the bus." Megan imitated pitch but used her own words.

Teacher melodically suggested "Let's go get candy." Not until candy was mentioned did all the children join in, singing about the kinds they would like. Lucas offered melody and words with a call every bit as lovely as the street cries of ancient vendors: "Red strawberries!"

He continued with: "Spencer's gonna buy candy bars. Hummmmm" (melodically for sound of bus motor). Lucas continued the musical play independently, ignoring teacher's comments to another child.

The play ended with a two-tone chant: "Get off . . . now, get off!" Teacher listened to the musical sounds and reinforced the idea by echoing the same words and pitches.

Musical Form within Improvisation

Rhyming

Children love the music of rhythm and rhyme.

With the use of rhyme, their songs begin to reflect organization. Older children no longer sing only through-composed melodies, for organized forms begin to appear. Rhythm and meter evolve through the natural use of word patterns; rhyming words at the end of the sentence begins to form a feeling of phrase. (A musical phrase is formed when a melodic idea seems to come to a pause or rest, about the length of one breath.) The use of pitch may be unintentionally limited to two or three tones owing to concentration on rhythm and word problems. Help children add rhyming to their songmaking by using the following techniques.

1. Is This My Rose? Play this game with an individual or group. While singing, the teacher points to a part of the body that will be the rhyming word. The wrong question is deliberately asked.

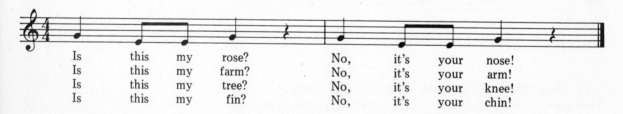

Is	this	my	rose?	No,	it's	your	nose!
Is	this	my	farm?	No,	it's	your	arm!
Is	this	my	tree?	No,	it's	your	knee!
Is	this	my	fin?	No,	it's	your	chin!

Another rhyming game may be played in the reading corner.

2. Michael Finnegan The delight of boys and girls in nonsense rhymes is reflected by the many examples found in our heritage of children's songs.

Michael Finnegan

Energetic

F

1. There was an old man named Mi - chael Fin - ne - gan,
2. There was an old man named Mi - chael Fin - ne - gan,

C7   **F**

He had whisk - ers on his chin - ne - gan, A - long came the wind and
He kicked up an aw - ful din - ne - gan, Be - cause they___ said he

                             C7   **F**

blew them in a - gain, Poor old Mi - chael Fin - ne - gan, Be - gin a - gain.
must not sing a - gain, Poor old Mi - chael Fin - ne - gan, Be - gin a - gain.

3. There was an old man named Michael Finnegan,
   He went fishing with a pinnegan,
   Caught a fish and dropped it in again,
   Poor old Michael Finnegan.
   Begin again.

4. There was an old man named Michael Finnegan,
   He grew fat and then grew thin again,
   Then he died and had to begin again,
   Poor old Michael Finnegan.
   Begin again.

Observing Children Learn

Teacher and Gina were in the reading corner looking at a picture containing a spoon, a balloon, the moon, and an abstract figure. They began to singsong:

Teacher (pointing to a balloon)   "Is this a spoon?"

Gina   "No, a balloon."

Teacher (pointing to the spoon)   "Is this a tune?"

Gina   "No, a spoon."

Teacher (pointing to moon)   "Is this a globy-bloon?"

Gina   "No, it's a moon."

The game continued, with teacher and child exchanging roles. The questions became sillier and sillier.

Gina (pointing to the moon)   "Is this a shobby-shoon?"

Teacher (looking in great disbelief)   "No, it's a moon!"

These words provoked even more nonsense rhymery. Gales of laughter permeated the song game.

Teacher enjoyed the rhyming games as thoroughly as did Gina. The facial and vocal responses of the teacher provided the child with the needed guarantee that efforts at playfulness are valued.

Children like their rhyming to be frequent. In most of their songs, rhyming tends to occur in consecutive lines. The following song lyrics were composed by four-year-old Cathy as she responded to a page from the singsong book. The song melodically began in the style of a through-composed song, but then began to take the shape of phrases due to the pattern of rhyming and the need to take a breath.

Cathy's Song

There was a little chicken.
It was sleeping one summer day;
It was fast asleep in the hay.
He said, "I'll sleep here today,
Guess I won't go away
Right here this very day."

3. Playground Rhyming   The teacher capable of modeling rhyming is most fortunate for much spontaneous play can evolve with teacher initiating such song.

Four-year-old Derek discovered new jumping equipment on the playground, a tire with canvas tautly stretched over the inner hole. The tire was placed flat on the ground, thus becoming a small trampoline. After Derek and other children had bounced several times, the teacher entered the play and improvised a rhyming song. Holding Derek's hand as he jumped, the teacher sang;

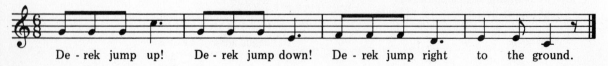

De - rek jump up!   De - rek jump down!   De - rek jump right   to   the ground.

Others quickly joined the game:

> Sherry, jump up! Sherry, jump down!
> Sherry can jump to the ground.

A long line of children repeated the game several times. The teacher used rhyming as a fun part of the game and also to reinforce the understanding of such words as "up" (high) and "down" (low).

Nonsense Songs

Children struggle to understand the world and to find just the right words to communicate understandings of objects, people, and functions. As a part of testing their new-found knowledge, they take great delight in changing known information into "opposites." They collapse into fits of gleeful laughter when a story, poem, or song suggests that the cat says, "Bow-wow," and the dog says, "Meow."

Nonsense ideas provide a great resource for song improvisation.

I know a hen that says, "Moo! Moo!" or *I know a cow that says "Cluck! Cluck!"*

Children all cry, "No, no, no, no. . . ."

These nonsense "opposite" games are played only when children are secure about their knowledge of whatever is being mixed up. The purpose is to teach, not confuse. If these improvisations are used in the appropriate manner, girls and boys soon fall into the fun of the game. They begin to test teacher on the ". . . pig that went for a ride in an old man's hat!"

Song literature reflects the child's delight through the ages with nonsense songs.

Shanghai Chicken

Shang-hai chick-en and he grow so tall, Hoo-day! Hoo-day!

Take that egg a month to fall, Hoo-day! Hoo-day!

Fantasy is important for children as they strive to gain mastery over their environment. It not only stretches and demands a great deal of creative thinking, but also allows the individual a feeling of great power. The self in the child becomes big and important. Fantasy becomes an unending resource for texts in vocal improvisation. The only limitations are the child's own concept and knowledge of the world. Creativity will come to a standstill if the teacher sings about something with which the child has had no contact.

Creating Songs within a Feeling of Tonality

A feeling of tonality is established when a series of tones or chords relate to a focal point. This focal point might be a single pitch around which other tones pivot, like a repeated melodic pattern or the first step of a scale. The harmonic accompaniment may also establish a tonal center, for the melody often uses tones from within the chords. Harmony will help determine whether the tonality will be major or minor.

The child begins to exhibit an awareness of tonality when singing improvisations using **simple repeated melodic patterns** and **harmonic accompaniments.**

1. *Simple Repeated Patterns* The teacher uses two-tone or three-tone chants as well as the through-composed melodies to model songmaking. This modeling is one way to give children a feeling of tonality. The teacher uses those tonal patterns found in the chants used by children at play:

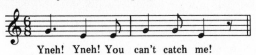

Yneh! Yneh! You can't catch me!

Children manipulate these pitches to create their own jingles. The use of set pitch intervals, rhythmic organization, and pattern repetition indicate growing structure in songmaking.

When motivating this kind of improvisation, the teacher may begin on a suitable pitch established by the child but use the following pitch relationships:

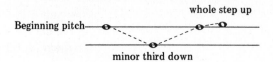

These pitches could be within this range:

G   E   G   A

If the child is singing in a lower range, they might be here:

F   D   F   G

The relationship of the pitches in the pattern will be the same even if the beginning pitch is higher or lower.

2. *Prerecorded Harmonic Accompaniments* The teacher may tape an ensemble playing several different *ostinato* accompaniments (short repeated melodic or rhythmic patterns).

Mallet-type or other available melodic instruments may be used. When recording, repeat the pattern many times so that there will be approximately three minutes of each example. Include several different examples on the same cassette tape.

The tape serves as the accompaniment for songmaking. The child operates the cassette at will, singing and playing improvised songs within the feeling of tonality established by the sounds of the instruments. Improvisations are relatively easy as the repeated patterns on tape are so predictable.

Following are examples of ensemble patterns that could be recorded:

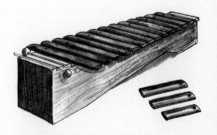

Bass xylophone

Soprano glockenspiel

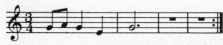

Alto glockenspiel

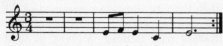

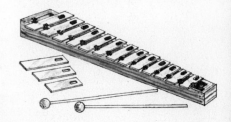

3. *Chordal Accompaniments* Use the guitar or Autoharp as an accompanying instrument. Play only one chord, such as C major or E minor, over and over as simple melodies are improvised.

Observing Children Learn

Teacher was holding the guitar as she sat on the rug. Surrounding her was a masking-taped circle she called a "hole." As children arrived that morning, they passed the "hole" to hang up their coats. One by one they passed, some stopping on their way, others looking quizzically at the teacher and the instrument. Randy asked, "What ya' doing?" Without waiting for an answer, he pointed to the guitar and said, "I can make sounds on that." Teacher answered, "I thought you might like to do that, Randy, so I made this hole for us to sit in while we play our music." Randy joined teacher in the hole and began strumming and plucking sounds on the guitar. (Before this, children had investigated the sounds of the guitar.) Other children now clustered near the edge of the hole and wanted to play at the same time. After the teacher explained that there could be only so many children in the "hole" at one time, they agreed to take turns. Each child played at random for a brief time; then teacher began to sing a simple two-tone melodic idea compatible with the E-minor chord sounds of the guitar.

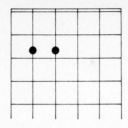

E-minor chord

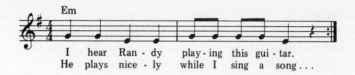

I hear Ran - dy play - ing this gui - tar.
He plays nice - ly while I sing a song...

(No effort was made to rhyme, but one could have been.)

Randy began singing, choosing his own pitches, but basically singing within the tonality of the E-minor chord he was playing. Teacher held the finger position for the chord while the children strummed.

Others were eager for a turn. Responses ranged from singing within to no concern for tonality. Some children just strummed or plucked and sang their own rambling tune. Throughout several weeks of repetition, the number of children singing in tune with the chord increased.

Improvisational Skills in Group Play

Older Threes and Fours show the desire and ability to function with others in group improvisations. The children create, using their skills both in through-composed and in simple patterned melodies. Improvisations within the group setting often involve two problems: maintaining the interest of the group when one child is improvising, and motivating the individual to improvise within the setting. One solution to the first problem is to give the group responsibility for a melodic idea that is to be repeated intermittently throughout the song. They must listen carefully to learn when they will be singing since the improvisor may perform a short or long musical idea. Individual improvisation may be initiated by the group or teacher asking a question. Encouraging each child to make up a song is easier if much singsong play has previously taken place.

1. Yellow Bug **This approach is suitable for large-group improvisations. When children gather in the assembly area, all sing the following two-tone song:**

See the lit - tle yel - low bug, He is un - der the
yel - low rug, What do you think he sees (Bob - by)?

What do you think he sees, Bobby?

The teacher encourages Bobby to sing his answer. Bobby's response may be within the two pitches sung in the question or in the style of a through-composed melody.

"I think he sees a big rock!"

The large group sings the question to Lela. Lela answers:

"He sees mother sweeping with a broom and she swishes him out of the room!"

The question is again sung by the group. Roger answers in a through-composed style, picking up Lela's ideas.

"She sweeps him away and he gets mashed up and mother says, 'I'm sorry' and he says put a bandage on me and take me to the hospital."

As is clear, this answer can wander, becoming every bit as dramatic as an adult tragic opera.

2. Let's Make an Opera The group sings *Let's Make an Opera*. Two or more children conversationally sing a song about any topic they choose. When the two soloists run out of ideas, the large group again sings, "Let's make. . . ." The game continues with different soloists.

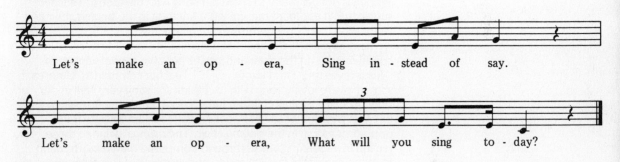

Let's make an op - era, Sing in - stead of say.

Let's make an op - era, What will you sing to - day?

3. Ask a Question

Teacher sings:

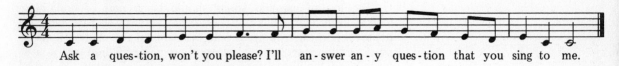

Ask a ques-tion, won't you please? I'll an-swer an-y ques-tion that you sing to me.

Child (through-composed melody) "Do you have a daddy?"

Teacher (answers using the child's style) "Yes, I have a nice daddy. He lives in a city far away."

Teacher sings original melody, and another question and answer are sung.

4. The Singing Chair Place a fancy chair in the large group assembly area. It may be an old dining room chair with an upholstered seat, any chair more ornate than normally found in a classroom. Shorten the legs so that it is child-height. In the child's eyes, the chair is now very special and thronelike. It should not remain in the area all year but only for a span of several weeks.

Observing Children Learn

The children gather on the rug. The singing chair is new to the environment. Teacher informs the children that this is a special chair, a place where children can sit and sing a song for others to hear. When a child sits in this chair to sing, other children will sit very quietly and listen.

"Who would like to sit in the singing chair?"

Amy, one of the more aggressive children, volunteers delightedly. She uses the first moments to feel the edges of the seat with her hands, wiggling to feel the softness of the seat on her bottom and twisting to see the back of the chair. After a moment, teacher redirects Amy's attention by saying, "Now that you are sitting on the singing chair, what song will you sing for us?" After a bit of coaxing, Amy, with eyes on the floor, sings a very soft, through-composed song of her own making.

Teacher invites Wanda to sit on the singing chair. Wanda shyly approaches the chair, half-sits and half-leans on it, not taking her feet from the floor. After a few moments, it becomes apparent that Wanda is not yet ready to share her song with the group. Teacher suggests that another time she will want to sit in the singing chair and share. Wanda happily returns to the group.

Andrea darts to the chair, squealing, "My turn! My turn!" Andrea confidently sits in the chair and begins her own special version of "Jesus loves me, This I know. . . ." Teacher comments, "Andrea shared a very lovely song with us. I think she sang very well in our singing chair." Not all children participated during the first session, but over a period of several weeks many took advantage of the opportunity to sit in the singing chair. Their songs included those recited in a speaking voice, through-composed melodies, rhyming tunes, variations of familiar tunes, and also accurate performances of familiar tunes. Teacher's musical questions were often enough to motivate the child's song.

The joy of creating songs should be a part of continuing education through adulthood, not merely an early-stage activity. An improvisation often requires only moments of the allotted time for music. Within a sequentially planned program, children will grow to understand the more sophisticated structure of music. They will become able to use such complex ideas of organization as planning melodic phrase endings with pitches that have a feeling of "finished or unfinished"; they will realize, that melodic phrases may be repeated in the same or slightly altered manner and that it is exciting to have same and different phrases within the melody. These are but a few of the skills and understandings that children will acquire and apply to their own improvised and composed songs.

Singing the Structured Songs of Others

Involvement in the structured vocal experience comes with increased social awareness and need for group-oriented activities. Participating within a group indicates a togetherness of action; thus, tone matching becomes important. To this point, we have carefully allowed the children to control the way they use their voices. We have provided many opportunities for vocal improvisation, both free and within the structure of tonality; we have continually modeled simple melodic ideas that may or may not have been imitated; and as a part of the environmental settings, we have presented many auditory experiences dealing with tonal discrimination. Now the child should be ready to perform more structured music—to cope with the language of the song, to hear and match pitches, sing specific intervals, discriminate between longer and shorter sounds and sing these in simple rhythmic combinations.

The child first chooses to sing selected fragments from the more structured songs presented. Such fragments are usually tonal patterns within a limited range often repeated. Their choice will probably be based on interest, language, and the child's ability to imitate musically. The child may be perceiving all parts of the song, actively participating by listening to word ideas, aware of the many contrasts in the music (rhythm, melody, volume), but singing only chosen parts.

The child's pitch may not be accurate; words may be chanted more than sung. Typically, upon hearing the teacher sing a song, the three-year-old sings his own version in response. The teacher should accept the child's version without insisting on precise imitation. The teacher has a song and the child has a song, too.

When children are developing the ability to perform music with others, hearing and accurately reproducing become necessary. During improvised song play, choices and decisions were made to satisfy the personal use of music. Using music socially, however, requires an agreement as to oneness of sound at a given time. The ability to match tones and rhythms is a part of a natural transition for many children. Other children need more time and experience to acquire skills for in-tune singing.

Responding to Rhythm in Melody

In improvisational activities, rhythmic concerns have been chiefly those inherent in improvised rhyming and movement experiences. In the more precise performance of a song, the duration of given tones becomes as important as the pitch. The child must now cope simultaneously with both rhythm and melody. One way to introduce melodic rhythm is to use the child's playground chants; explore the rhythm patterns of the words in relation to the underlying beat. Later these same ideas may be explored through the rhythm pattern of words in the melody.

When combining chanting and movement, the child deals with several factors:

1. Voice inflection;
2. Feeling of phrase;
3. Rhythm patterns of the words;
4. Meter;
5. Relationship of the underlying beat.

Chants should begin simply, contain repetition, and be brief, perhaps no more than two lines long. Rhymes may include nonsense elements and be accompanied by body movements prescribed by child or adult. Chanting games used on the playground or in the classroom should involve large body movements with occasional use of small muscle actions.

Children naturally tend to do more than one thing at a time and should be encouraged to do so. Various coordination skills of clapping, patting, or jumping while simultaneously chanting provide a most logical basis on which to develop rhythmic skills. As coordination skills increase, the performance of more complex rhythmic and melodic ideas takes place.

Combine clapping and walking so that the body is more totally involved; then add a chant. Walking need not proceed in a formal circle, for this only adds an unnecessary element of structure. The rule is to walk only in the places where there are no other children.

The following examples for setting chants are usable with pre-school children. Additional examples may be found in such literature as nursery rhymes and jump-rope and other game chants or may be created by teacher's own rhyming efforts.

1. The Cow

Movement **Clap and walk a steady beat.**

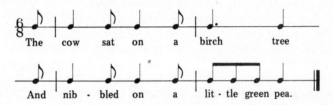

Movement stops abruptly. Shake head while speaking with voice inflection: "Nibblety-nibblety-nibblety . . . nib!" Repeat chant several times. Model different body positions when stopping to "nibble."

2. Special Voices
Accompaniment **Clap a steady beat.**

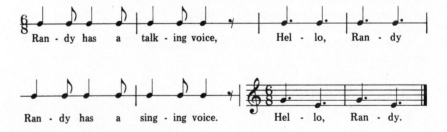

3. Intry Mintry
Movement **Walk and clap a basic beat. Pantomime motions are indicated by words.**

In - try Min - try wig - gle an eye,

Poke your nose and tic - kle a fly!

For variation, sit at table or on rug. Use desk bell (with plunger level). Sing with one child.

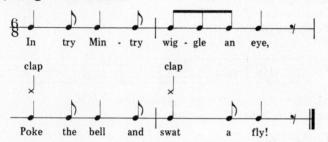

In try Min - try wig - gle an eye,

clap   clap

Poke the bell and swat a fly!

4. Ring the Bell

Place a desk bell on the floor in the middle of a circle of standing children. Walk rhythmically to one child while chanting:

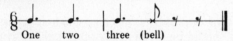

Ring the bell with me

Take one of the child's hands and walk with the steady beat to the bell. Child steps on bell plunger to make sound while teacher helps him balance:

One   two   three (bell)

Move back rhythmically to place while chanting:

The bell went ring - a - lee,   One two three!

Repeat by choosing other children from circle.

5. Gypsy Ipsy
Movement Walk a steady beat.

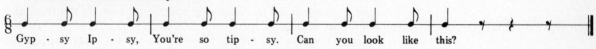

Gyp - sy Ip - sy, You're so tip - sy. Can you look like this?

Movement stops and child assumes the funniest position possible.

Repeat, finding different ways to stop each time.

Tempo is critical to the successful performance of a movement chant. The teacher should be sensitive to any pressures children experience as a result of performing too fast or too slowly. An overly slow tempo is difficult for a young child as it necessitates holding and balancing, which require refined coordination skills.

Matching Tones   Any of the chants that the children have now learned may be changed from speaking to two- or three-tone singing.

1. Gypsy Ipsy

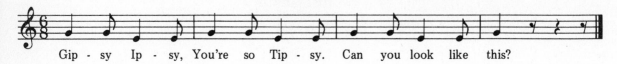

Gip - sy Ip - sy, You're so Tip - sy.   Can   you look like   this?

2. The Cow

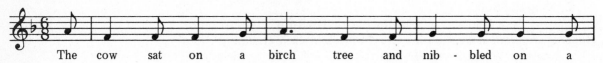

The   cow   sat   on   a   birch   tree   and   nib - bled   on   a

lit - tle   green   pea   a   nib - ble - ty,   nib - ble - ty . . .

There is no **one** approach to teaching children accuracy in tone matching. They should be given many opportunities to practice by singing with others. Limiting the pitches initially is a logical help. Also, one might begin with patterns that use the higher pitch first, allowing the voice to descend effortlessly to the lower pitch. The child will tend to explode air initially on the first tone, leaving less breath available for the second. A pattern that moves from low to high gives the higher tone less air support, decreasing the chance of accurate matching. Once the pitches are experienced in place, the continuous flow within the melodic line is likelier to be accurate.

Body movements can assist the child in tone matching. When performing two-tone songs, play games that utilize arms in an up-and-down position relative to specific pitches. When the child pulls arms slightly up, lungs are filled; chest is expanded; the body is ready to produce the sound. Consistently use the same movement with a specific pitch so that the child may experience a concrete kinesthetic association with the abstract vocal placement of a given pitch.

The following body signals may be used for pitches that are found in the child's natural chanting games.

1. Echo Song

Yoo hoo! How are you?

Touch top of head.

Touch shoulders

Fingers pointed up over head

2. Rain, Rain

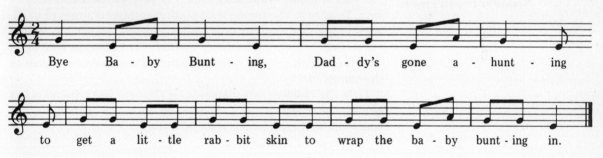

Rain rain go a-way, Come a-gain an-oth-er day.

Use the same large body movements when singing these songs.

3. Bye Baby Bunting

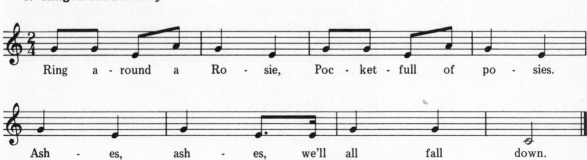

Bye Ba-by Bunt-ing, Dad-dy's gone a-hunt-ing

to get a lit-tle rab-bit skin to wrap the ba-by bunt-ing in.

4. Ring Around a Rosy

Ring a-round a Ro-sie, Poc-ket-full of po-sies.

Ash-es, ash-es, we'll all fall down.

Children soon sing songs that contain a variety of pitches, but wide, awkward intervals and range continue to pose problems. Basic music textbooks for the kindergarten level include songs within a suitable range and appropriate teaching suggestions. This broad selection of songs helps us meet our responsibility to expose children to music of many cultures, times, and places.

Song Resources

The following examples of songs and teaching guides are from various textbook series. Through the song, children learn such concepts as melodic direction and patterns, phrases, dynamics, steady beat, and rhythm. The information is packaged in a playful manner appropriate to the child's mode of learning. Useful song resources are listed in the bibliography (page 193).

1. Johnny, Get Your Hair Cut

Key: B♭   Starting Tone: B♭   Meter $\frac{2}{4}$

Learnings and Skills

The student should be able to:
*1. Sing a song at various dynamic levels.
  2. Create a "sound effect" and/or instrumental accompaniment.

Student Involvement

*1. This is a very short song which is easy to learn and easy to sing. To vary it, try singing it through a number of times (3 or 4), each time softer than the time before until the last verse is simply "mouthed." To vary it further, "mouth" the last verse until "just like me" which may be sung or spoken. Does everyone finish at the same time?
2. Help the children select sounds for clippers and scissors (sand blocks, vocal sounds, etc.) and use the sounds to accompany the song—or by themselves as a sound piece.

Related Activities

1. Poetry: "Hippety Hop to the Barber Shop," Mother Goose, and "Barber's Clippers" by Dorothy Baruch, both in *The Sound of Poetry* by Mary C. Austin and Queenie B. Mills. Boston: Allyn and Bacon, Inc., 1963: "Barber, Barber, Shave a Pig" in *Barnes Book of Nursery Verse* by Barbara Ireson. New York: A. S. Barnes & Co., 1960.
2. Book: *Billy the Barber* by Dorothy Kunhardt. New York: Harper and Row, 1961.
3. Finger play: "Snip, Snip, Snip, Snippety" in *Let's Do Fingerplays* by Marion Grayson. Washington: Robert B. Luce, Inc., 1962.

Johnny, Get Your Hair Cut

Well accented

Folk Song

John-ny get your hair cut, hair cut, hair cut, John-ny get your hair cut, just like me!

2. Hickory, Dickory, Dock

Purpose   To use the woodblock for sound effects with a song.

Materials   Recording, woodblocks, triangle of finger cymbal, bells.

Motivation   Say the Mother Goose rhyme *Hickory, Dickory, Dock*.

Exploration   Have the children:

1. Listen to the song. Imagine they hear a clock ticking.
2. Listen again and move their arms like the pendulum of a large clock. (Show a picture of a clock with a pendulum if unfamiliar to children.)
3. Play a "tick-tock" accompaniment with the song. (A single woodblock may be used throughout the song, or a high-pitched block may be used for "tick" and a lower-pitched one for "tock.")
4. Add other sound effects, such as striking "one" on a triangle or finger cymbals, and playing a descending glissando (slide) on the bells when the mouse runs down the clock.

Desired Responses   The children should show increasing ability to play woodblocks and move to the pulse of the song (on the first and fourth beats of each measure), build an imaginative accompaniment of sound effects with other instruments, and sing with increasing pitch and rhythmic accuracy.

Hickory, Dickory, Dock

Wood Block

Music by J. W. Elliot Mother Goose Rhyme

Hick - o - ry, dick - o - ry, dock, The mouse ran up the clock; The clock struck one, The mouse ran down; Hick - o - ry, dick - o - ry, dock.

3. Knock at the Door

Key: G   Starting Tone: B   Meter: $\frac{6}{8}$

Learnings and Skills The student should be able to:

1. Create actions to accompany a song.

2. Imitate rhythm patterns found in the song

3. Create a "sound story."

4. Create a 4-tone song.

1. Ask the class to listen carefully to the words and tell how many different things the words tell them to do.
2. Play the melody on a set of melody bells held vertically. How many notes are used in the song? (4)
3. Let the children experiment with the four tones G, A, B, D to discover what kind of "songs" they can make.
4. There are 3 distinct rhythm patterns in this song. Once the children have learned the song well, use each or all of the patterns as rhythmic introductions, accompaniments or interludes. Play each pattern with a different rhythm instrument, if possible.

Knock at the Door

Traditional

Knock at the door! Peep in! Pull the latch and walk in!

4. Teddy Bear*

Key: B♭   Starting Tone: B♭   Meter $\frac{2}{4}$

PITCH: Tones in a melody pattern may move from high to low or from low to high.

Concept

Play this melody pattern on the bells.

Discover

Ask children to show how the pattern moves with their hands. DOES IT GO UP OR DOWN? LISTEN CAREFULLY. HOW MANY TIMES DO YOU HEAR THIS PATTERN IN THE SONG? (Four times; once at the beginning of each phrase.) Provide bells   and G and give different children the opportunity to play the pattern each time it occurs while the class sings the song.

STRUCTURE: Melodies are made up of smaller sections called phrases.

Discover

Some children will already know this rhyme from their jumping games. Make up motions as an aid to remembering the words. Remind them that they should plan a new motion for each new phrase. The motions might be as follows.

Other Concept

Teddy Bear

1. Ted-dy Bear, Ted-dy Bear, turn a-round,_ Ted-dy Bear, Ted-dy Bear, touch the ground.
2. Ted-dy Bear, Ted-dy Bear, go up-stairs,_ Ted-dy Bear, Ted-dy Bear, say your prayers.

Ted-dy Bear Ted-dy Bear, show your shoe,_ Ted-dy Bear, Ted-dy Bear, that will do.
Ted-dy Bear, Ted-dy Bear, switch off the light,_ Ted-dy Bear, Ted-dy Bear, say "Good Night."

5. The Old Gray Cat

Key: C   Starting Tone: C   Meter: $\frac{2}{4}$ $\frac{6}{8}$

What are some of the things that the mice do in this song?
Creep, nibble, scamper

What does the cat do?
Sleeps, creeps

To help the children learn the order or sequence of the verses, make flannel cutouts, or let the children help draw pictures to represent each of the events in the song. Display the appropriate cutout or picture as the children sing each verse. This is a good technique to use for songs that have many verses.

Let the children take turns acting out one of the verses for others to identify. Another time, encourage the children to take turns playing the bells on "in (through) the house" when others sing. Line up three bells—low E, F, and G—and have the children discover which *direction* to play. (Upward)

After the children have had several experiences with "The Old Gray Cat," do *Crayon Activity Twenty-three.*

Each picture shows what happens in one of the verses of the song. For this activity, the children put the pictures in the proper order or sequence by drawing a line from the number 1 to the picture that shows what happens first; from the number 2 to the picture that shows what happens second; and so forth. An activity such as this provides a way to evaluate children's auditory memory.

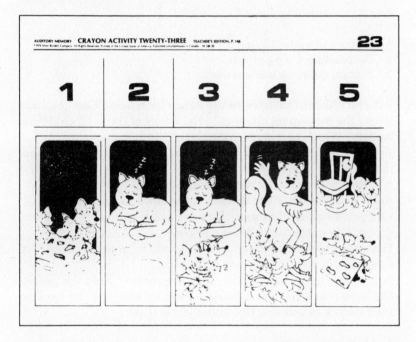

The Old Gray Cat

Traditional American Song
Arranged by Cameron McGraw

Freely

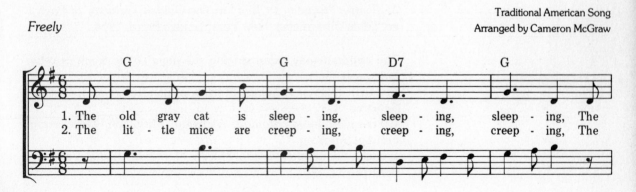

1. The old gray cat is sleep - ing, sleep - ing, sleep - ing, The
2. The lit - tle mice are creep - ing, creep - ing, creep - ing, The

old gray cat is sleep - ing in the house._____
lit - tle mice are creep - ing through the house._____

6. How Many Days Has My Baby to Play?

Key: C   Starting Tone: C   Meter: $\frac{2}{4}$ $\frac{6}{8}$

Music Learnings 1. Change of meter ($\frac{2}{4}$ and $\frac{6}{8}$)
2. Descending scale pattern
3. Textual question and answer

Child Involvement Ask the children to listen to the song. Then ask: "Can you hear where the movement changes? Which part of the song could you walk to? Which part could you skip to?"
Ask: "What question does the song ask? Does this question come in the first or second part of the song? Is there an answer? What is it? In what part of the song does it come?"
Ask: "Can you hear the melody come down in part of the song? Can you sing just that part? Can you show with your hand how the melody comes down? Can you play it on the bells?"
Have the children make up a new melody by going up from C to C, instead of down in this part of the song.
Ask: "How many days of the week are there?" Sing the part of the song that tells this. Have the class try to count the days on their fingers as you sing the names of the days.

Related Activities 1. Music: Have the class review "The Mulberry Bush." Have them sing and dramatize it.
2. Language: Ask the children to bring calendars from home and have them find the names of the days of the week.
3. Poetry: "Sunday's Child" in *The Golden Treasury of Poetry*, ed. Louis Untermeyer, New York: Golden Press, 1964.

The children may enjoy singing the days of the week in other languages.
Spanish: *Domingo, Lunes, Martes, Miércoles, Jueves, Viernes, Sábado.*
German: *Sonntag, Montag, Dienstag, Mittwoch, Donnerstag, Freitag, Samstag.*
French: *Dimanche, Lundi, Mardi, Mercredi, Jeudi, Vendredi, Samedi.*

How Many Days Has My Baby to Play?

Mother Goose Rhyme
Music by Edna Henrietta Becker

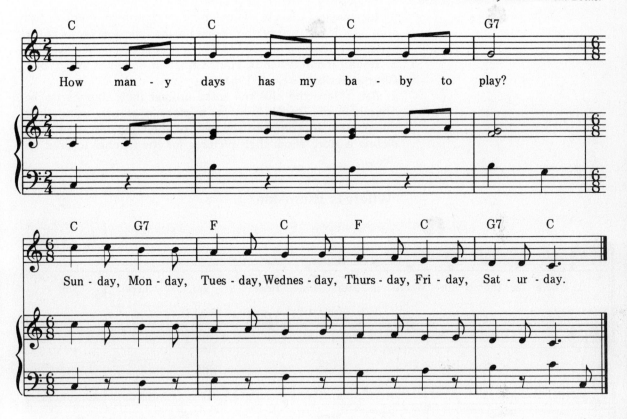

How man - y days has my ba - by to play?

Sun - day, Mon - day, Tues - day, Wednes - day, Thurs - day, Fri - day, Sat - ur - day.

7. Where Is Thumbkin?

Key: F   Starting Tone: F   Meter: $\frac{4}{4}$

1. Repetition of melodic patterns
2. Chord outline: *F-A-C*

Music Learnings

Ask the children to listen for the repeated melody patterns. It may be helpful to isolate measures 1-2, 3-4, 5-6, 7-8.

Child Involvement

Hand out the *F, A* and *C* resonator bells, or play these pitches on the songbells or piano when they occur on the first beat of each measure.

Play all three tones simultaneously. Use this *F-A-C* as an accompaniment for the entire song.

After the children become familiar with the song, ask them what the song does when they finish singing about one finger and start singing about another. Lead them to the realization that the whole song is repeated for each verse.

Related Activities   1. Fingerplay: Do the fingerplay while singing the song.
2. Language: Discuss the meaning of *Thumbkin, Pointer, Tall Man,* etc. Have the children listen for the repeated words in the song.
3. Book: *Thumbelina* by Hans Christian Andersen. New York: Charles Scribner's Sons, 1961.
4. Art: Have the children trace around their thumbs (to be Thumbkin or Thumbelina) on a piece of paper, using their imagination to complete the rest of their picture. They may dictate a story about their pictures for the teacher to print on them.

Where Is Thumbkin?

Traditional Song

2. Where is pointer?   4. Where is ring man?
3. Where is tall man?   5. Where is little man?
6. Where's the family? (Here we are)

8. Andrew Mine, Jasper Mine

What are some of the names of children you know?
Listen for the names of the children in this song.

Clap the **rhythm pattern** made by the words "Andrew mine" and "Jasper mine."

Take time to experiment with the names of children in the group. Which names have the same pattern? Examples: Jeffrey mine, Laura mine, Elsie mine

Andrew Mine, Jasper Mine

Moravian Carol
Arranged by Rosemary Jacques
English Words by C. K. Offer

Joyously

Summary Add the expressive elements of music to language and song emerges. Singing is a joyful natural activity. Children need little incentive to create their own songs or to perform those of others.

Children should be encouraged to use their voices for "musical scribbling." The art teacher would not expect three- to five-year-old children to copy a picture of a squirrel; rather, this teacher would invite children to create their own picture of a squirrel. So it is with music: children should not be asked merely to copy another's song; the setting should be such that they create their own.

The child's improvisations will blossom in an environment where loved adults approve and value music-making efforts. Thoughtless ridicule or statements like, "That's enough noise!" from such important people can quickly halt creativity.

Through a sequential process, boys and girls grow in ability to perform the music of others. The significance of the present approach in contrast to others is that the child **evolves to** the stage of performing another's song instead of beginning with total imitation. If the process has been effective, the child is better prepared for songmaking through these improvements:

1. More skills and understandings of the way music is organized;
2. Increased control of the voice;
3. Courage to make judgments regarding songmaking;
4. Greater value for own creative efforts;
5. More skillful performance of composed songs.

Playing with Sound-making Objects 5

Did you hear that bug?
He's my friend, ya know.

He buzzed at me fifty times;

Then I saw him go.

Children are bombarded with a cacophony of sounds, and as soon as they begin to listen and determine relationships, the world of sound affects their learning. Researchers have noted that babies react to sounds shortly after birth. Within the first year, the baby is able to discriminate between pitches and to localize sounds.

Children learn about sound in four steps:

1. They become aware that sounds exist.
2. They learn that there are differences between sounds.
3. They discover that they can make sounds like those they hear.
4. They realize that sounds can be organized to communicate ideas and feelings.

From early infancy, the child needs many sounds in the environment. At first, the child produces random sounds on various objects, learning by touching and seeing as well as by hearing. Even the senses of taste and smell may come into play as mallets and other instruments are tested to see if they could possibly be good to eat. Initially, the child bangs, hits, and flails away at the sound-making objects. Later, the child refines motor actions, begins to listen more carefully, and then finds reasons to use the sounds in specific ways.

Through manipulation of concrete objects, the child establishes visual images as well as making sound associations. By verbalizing, the child acquires language to deal more effectively with future sound encounters. Learning requires this type of active manipulation for meaning to evolve.

Within this chapter, we will take the child from the stage of raucous, free exploration of sounds to that of playing simple patterns on instruments. We shall describe teacher-made environments and sound studies to be placed within these environments, and we shall examine the rationale for each experience as it relates to growth in musical understandings.

Musical Reasons for Sound Exploration

Inherent in this program is the basic philosophy that there is a body of knowledge about music to be acquired by children. Within each experience, the child will deal with basic music understandings.

Though the child may not be fully cognizant of the given musical concept being presented, the teacher must be. It is through this awareness that the teacher can plan a sequential, meaningful, and enjoyable course of learning. Each experience should contribute to the child's growing awareness and ability to make decisions about music.

Children respond initially to the totality of music. They move to music, expressing that aspect upon which their attention may be fleetingly directed. They may respond to rhythm or articulation of sound, to timbres, pitch changes, or perhaps all of these combined. Children do not knowingly isolate or verbally communicate about specific ideas within the musical selection. It is through observing their movements that the teacher gains a clue to what the children hear.

A child who is not ready to abstract specific sounds from within an ensemble may begin to deal more knowingly with a given idea by "centering" on a single sound:

A SINGLE BELL

Musical concepts inherent in exploring the sound of a bell are these:

1. **Timbre** A bell has a ringing sound.
2. **Duration** It can ring for a long or short time.

3. **Volume** Its sound can be loud or soft and can gradually change between these two qualities.

The child begins at the perceptual level, then builds more sophisticated ideas about specific sounds. Understanding of music concepts may evolve through the following levels over a long period of time.

The purpose of the early-childhood experience is to introduce basic ideas. These and more in-depth learnings will be reinforced throughout the elementary-school music experience.

Basic Music Concepts   Level 1

Timbre	Sounds have distinctive characteristic qualities
Duration	Sounds may be relatively long or short
Pitch	Sounds may be relatively high or low
Volume	Sounds are relatively loud or soft
Tempo	Sounds are relatively fast or slow
Form	Structure is determined by the manner in which musical ideas are combined.
Articulation	Sounds may be jagged and disconnected or smooth and flowing
Expressive Tonality	All elements combined to express a musical or nonmusical idea

---

Basic Music Concepts   Level 2

Timbre	When instruments are played in different ways, they produce different timbres.
Duration	Music moves with an underlying beat.
Pitch	Sounds may be repeated, move up, or move down.
Volume	Dynamics is a change in volume. Sounds may gradually become louder or softer. Sounds may quickly become louder or softer.
Tempo	Within a composition, tempo may change for a variety of expressive purposes.
Form	Musical form is determined by the use of repetition and contrast (whole – part, same – different).
Expressive Totality	All elements combined express a musical or nonmusical idea.

Basic Music Concepts   Level 3

Timbre	Interaction with prior concepts should be continued.
Duration	Rhythm is a grouping of longer or shorter sounds or silences. Rhythm may move evenly or unevenly in relation to the underlying beat.

Pitch	Melody is made up of a series of tones which may repeat or move up and down.
	Tones may move up or down by steps or skips.
	Two or more tones performed simultaneously produce harmony.
Volume	Interaction with prior concepts should be continued.
Tempo	Interaction with prior concepts should be continued.
Form	Interaction with prior concepts should be continued.
Expressive	
Totality	Interaction with prior concepts should be continued.

Sound Studies

In planned environments for sound explorations, the objects must be so sturdy that damage is unlikely. One of the purposes of the experience is to help the child develop approach tendencies toward music, and an unhappy experience resulting in a "broken" instrument does not lead to this goal. If the child is to explore freely, there cannot be cautions of "Don't hit too hard!" or "Watch out, it will break!" One concept to be discovered is that sounds may be loud or soft; thus, hitting "hard" may be important.

Besides being sturdily constructed, initial sound exploration environments should be large enough for the child to have a good playing surface and room for wide, swinging arm motions.

The teacher must be prepared for many sounds from the music area each time new materials are introduced. The first explorations are usually the most boisterous. When the children begin to deal with problem-solving ideas within the setting, their actions become more purposeful and controlled. The purpose of first encounters with sound studies is the children's perception and assimilation of a variety of musical sounds. Subsequent encounters with the same sound studies require children to discriminate about the sounds by ordering or classifying them.

The manipulatable objects are gradually scaled down as the children demonstrate greater ability to control small muscle movement. Traditional instruments are used whenever possible so that the teacher is not responsible for creating and constructing all sound sources. Smaller studies are pursued in such areas as the work tables, soft corner, on a small rug designated for music, or even outdoors.

When playing within the learning centers, children are left in control of how they interact with the materials. The teacher intervenes when appropriate, picking up cues from the children about how a given game will be played. With respect to even a single sound, usually more than one musical element is involved. The teacher may initially plan the study to encompass several music concepts or to focus on one predominant aspect.

The following materials describe typical sound studies, the music concepts to be explored, the environments to be created, the objectives of the study, the ways the play may proceed, teacher observations, and teacher comments with appropriate vocabulary.

These sound studies are to be viewed as **models** for exploratory experiences the teacher may devise. They are not listed in a sequence for presentation to children. The teacher should not hesitate to adapt the ideas rather than using them precisely as set forth here.

SOUND STUDY 1:   SANDPAPER WALL

Sounds may be combined to express a nonmusical idea like a story (*expressive totality*).
Sounds have distinctive characteristics and qualities (**timbre**).
Sounds are relatively loud or soft (**volume**).

Music Concepts

Sound box Cover a slide-in wall four feet square with sandpaper textures.

Sound Starters Cover two car-shaped blocks with coarse sandpaper and two small blocks with fine sandpaper; provide two small blocks that have no sandpaper covering.

Setting the Environment

Sound Box: Sandpaper Wall

Given an opportunity to interact in the environment, the child will produce and discover a variety of "scratchy, swishy" sounds and grow in awareness of similarities and differences in sounds.

Play The child will manipulate such sound starters as blocks shaped like cars, trucks, or in various geometric patterns. The child will use sounds expressively.

Observable Behaviors Does the child explore sounds at random?
Does the child try using each sound starter on sandpaper wall?
Does the child use sound expressively (pretend, for example, it is a car sound)?
Does the child imitate sounds of sandpaper blocks with vocal sounds?
Does the child seem aware of the differences in sounds of the various textures on the sandpaper wall?
Does the child use new or known music vocabulary when playing?

Appropriate Teacher Dialogue *Let me hear the sound your car (block, truck) makes.* (The term "noise" is not used.)

 Can you make a different sound with your car (block, truck)?
 (Child may choose another starter or go to a different texture on wall.)

Key words are "fast, slow" "loud, soft" "swish, scratch."

Games to Play Children make sounds using sound starters on wall:

1. Point to a place on sandpaper wall.
 Stuart, make a soft sound right here!
 Mike, make a long sound right here!
2. *Who can make many soft sounds to put baby to sleep? Loud sounds to wake baby?*
3. *The house is on fire. Make the "shhhhhh" sound of the water as it puts out the fire.*
4. *Make the soft sound while you sing a lullaby* (singsong tune).

Observing Children Learn

Today was the Threes' first experience in the sound box. Several children played in the area immediately. Some of the more aggressive boys were the first to enter. John, the leader of two other boys, said, "I think I'll go in there!" The others quickly followed. Their comments were, "This is my house . . . Let's be firemen. . . ." They soon discovered the sound starters and used them as toys, saying, "Choo, choo, choo!" No notice was taken of the sandpaper wall.

 They began to explore the box by moving carpet squares that had been placed on the floor for comfort. The sound starters were thumped on the squares and pushed through the holes in the top of the box. The boys decided to swing by dangling from the open areas in the top of the box. The teacher intervened, declaring this to be one way we do not play in the box.

The children began to explore sounds in a more organized manner when the teacher said, "This is a house in which to make sounds. Do you see the wall that is different?" The boys responded zestfully, making several vigorous passes with the sandpaper blocks. Shortly they left the area.

John returned three times to the box during the next thirty minutes. Upon each visit, he produced random sounds before leaving.

Other children entered the box, some remaining briefly, others poking heads in to take a look.

Brian sat at the table nearest the sound box, working a puzzle. He looked repeatedly at the box but did not enter. Later, John, Sue, and Raymond were playing in the box. The teacher entered into the activity, peeked in the doorway, and asked, "May I come in and play with you?" The children granted cautious permission. The game began:

Teacher   "Can you make soft sounds on the wall? Loud?" (Children did so with accuracy.)

Teacher   "Can you make fast sounds? Slow sounds?" (Again, very accurate responses.)

Randy joined the group.

Sue said, "I'll be the baby," and flopped down in a sleeping position.

Teacher   "That's a good idea. Let's put the baby to sleep."

John   "I'll go get the milk".

Others   "Me, too! Me, too!"

Out of the box they crawled, returning promptly with the make-believe milk. Teacher cupped her hands and said, "Pour it into my bottle." Children complied excitedly, using much pantomime.

Teacher   "Who can sing a song and make soft sounds to help put the baby to sleep?"

Randy   "I can." Very seriously Randy sang a lovely "go to sleep" song in singsong style. Others made soft sounds on the wall. The soft sounds didn't last long for John burst into loud banging sound.

Teacher   "Those were very loud sounds. I think the baby must be awake!"

The game became a favorite and had to be repeated many times. Randy continued to create melodies. Raymond, though in the box, sat and listened. He did not participate actively. The interest of the group began to wane, and the game was almost over when Raymond decided to singsong a lullaby. The other children were not paying attention, but Raymond didn't seem to notice. All soon left the box. The "put the baby to sleep" game was played on subsequent days with the same group and with new members who expressed interest.

While passing the box, the teacher overheard children saying,
"John, you make a loud sound!"

John, "Yeh!"

Another child "Hey! Make a soft sound!"

This dialogue did not continue beyond the two or three instructions at this time, but was noted as a significant musical behavior for Threes at play.

Activities with the sandpaper wall may be interspersed with other studies over several months. Upon observing a lessening in interest, the teacher may change the environment to provide another timbre or create new games to be played by slightly altering the same environment.

For example, using the same side or reversing the board to create a new work surface, the teacher can place hooks over six squares of coarse-textured sandpaper. Six puzzle cards are placed in the bottom of the box with one sound starter (a sandpaper block). The puzzle cards contain pictures of a cat purring and meowing (three each). The child's problem is to hang the puzzle cards on the hooks over sandpaper and then make loud or soft sounds appropriate to each picture.

SOUND STUDY 2:   SANDPAPER PUZZLE

Setting the Environment   Prepare a matching puzzle in which textures of sandpaper are placed on top of the puzzle pieces with like pieces to be fitted below. The texture pieces in the top row are the control pieces of the puzzle and should be placed on blocks of one color. Manipulatable working pieces are on a contrasting color. The puzzle can be constructed of masonite or plywood. Texture pieces are fitted into a box frame. Textures include two coarse sandpaper, two fine sandpaper, and two plain pieces representing the least sound of all.

Music Concepts   Sounds may be relatively loud or soft *(volume)*.
Sounds have distinctive characteristics *(timbre)*.
Objects that look alike may sound alike.

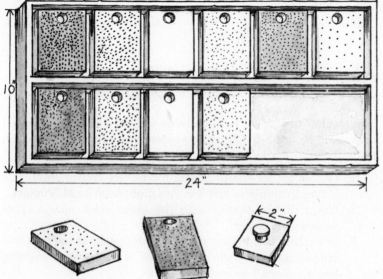

Given an opportunity to manipulate puzzle pieces using visual and auditory clues, the child will be able to match similar pieces.

Objectives of the Study

The puzzle board is placed on the work table with control pieces inserted and manipulatable working pieces scattered on the table. Teacher invites children to find a piece that looks and sounds the same as one to which she points. Upon visually matching textures, the child uses a sound starter to test if the two pieces sound the same before completing another part of the puzzle. Before each game, the teacher changes the order of the control pieces and again mixes up the working pieces. When they are able, two children play the game, and teacher leaves the area.

Play

Does the child successfully match pieces?
Does the child explore auditorily or rely only on visual clues when independently playing with the puzzle?

Observable Behaviors

Make references to loudness and softness or timbres as child matches pieces:

Appropriate Teacher Dialogue

Those both made loud, swishy, scratching sounds! They must be the same!
I heard hardly any sound at all; those were both so soft. They must be the same.
I wonder who can find this loud, scratchy sound?

Key Words are "loud and soft" (*volume*), "swishy and scratchy" (*timbre*), "same and different."

SOUND STUDY 3:   SOUND SHAKERS _____

Music Concepts

Sounds may be relatively louder or softer *(volume)*.
Sounds have distinctive characteristics and quality *(timbre)*.

Setting the Environment

The teacher of four- or five-year-olds will need to prepare sound sources to be used in different combinations as children proceed through these games.

1. Obtain six (or more) plastic pill bottles (approximately 2 inches in diameter and 3 inches high) from local druggist.
2. Cover all the bottles with the same color opaque pre-pasted shelf paper.
3. In each of two bottles place 1 inch of salt; in each of two bottles place 1 inch of rice, and in the two remaining bottles, place 1 inch of dried beans.
4. Glue caps on securely.
5. Prepare game sheets as shown.

The six sound containers will be adequate for the game sheets unless you wish to have all studies prepared in advance. If so, you will need additional containers for use by many children simultaneously.

Objectives of the Study

Given an opportunity to explore three contrasting volumes, the child will discriminate among soft, loud, and very loud using only aural (nonvisual) clues.

The child will demonstrate understanding by solving problems involving same and different, classifying as to softer or louder, judging appropriate use of volume to express ideas, and selecting appropriate volume to accompany three melodies.

Play

The containers and game sheets are placed in individual work areas. The child will play different games in this series, each sequentially requiring greater skill in discrimination. New games are introduced only when the teacher observes that the child is ready to proceed to more advanced problem-solving. The child will enjoy repeating the puzzles.

Observable Behaviors

Does the child seem to listen while shaking containers or merely make random decisions about sounds?

Does the child demonstrate ability to hear loud or soft sounds by appropriately placing containers on game sheets?

Does the child sustain interest in the activity? Demonstrate a need to progress to the next challenge level? Repeat the same level with different game sheets?

Listen to these sounds. Are they the same or different?
I hear rattling (swishing; loud; soft) sounds.

Key Words are "loud, soft, very loud," *(volume),*
"swish, rattling"   *(timbre),* "same and different."

Three sound choices: two soft, one very loud

*Game 1:   Same and
Different*

The child will determine which sounds are the same or different
by shaking the containers and will demonstrate understanding by
placing the two soft containers on the like faces and the very loud
container on the different face.

Observable Behaviors

The teacher should provide as little assistance as possible in the
problem-solving. Draw attention to the little boy on the study
sheet. Discuss what he is doing.

Can you do what the boy is doing? (Shake containers and
listen.) *Can you hear the sounds that are the same? Which are
different? After you have listened to the sounds, place them
on the faces that are the same or different.* Ask these
questions; then leave child to discover the answers independently. Return when the child has completed the puzzle.
Shake the containers to check findings.

*Appropriate Teacher
Dialogue*

It is possible to vary game sheets without increasing complexity
of problem.

Game 2: **Same and Different**   Four sound choices: two soft, two very loud

Observable Behaviors   The child will determine which sounds are the same or different by shaking the containers and will demonstrate understanding by placing the two soft sounds on the faces with small ears and closed eyes and the very loud sounds on the faces with large ears and open eyes.

Appropriate Teacher Dialogue   *Which sounds are the same? Shake the sounds to find out. Can you put the softest sounds on the sleepy face? The very loud sounds on the wide-awake faces?* Let the child complete the puzzle independently. Return later and shake the containers to check the findings.

Game 3: **Sound Story**   Two sound choices: one soft, one very loud

Observable Behaviors   The child will determine which sound is soft or very loud by shaking the containers. Using dialogue to tell what is happening to the children in the pictures, the child will add the appropriate sound while telling the story and place the correct sound shaker on each circle.

Appropriate Teacher Dialogue   *Which sound is very soft? Very loud? What kind of a sound would the little boy's sled make as it slides down the snowy hill? What kind of a sound would the boy's wagon make as it rolls down a bumpy hill? Use the loud or soft sounds to help tell about the snowy or rocky hill.*

Teacher may remain with child to hear this story, then suggest that the child leave the shakers on the game sheet for someone else to use.

Three sound choices: one soft, one loud, one very loud

The child will determine which sounds are soft, loud, and very loud. Place shakers on appropriate faces.

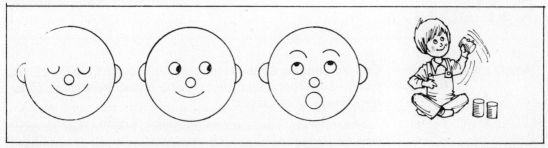

Shake the containers. Listen to the sounds. Which of the sounds is new? (Loud) Place this new sound on the face in the middle of the game sheet. Where could you place the softest sound? Very loudest sound?

Invite the child to help you tell a story. Teacher begins:
"A little boy named Billy was almost asleep. He heard a very soft sound (child shakes soft container) but it didn't wake him up (put shaker back on sleepy face).

"When Billy heard a louder sound (shake loud sound), he opened his eyes and said, 'I think I hear a loud sound, but where did it come from?'" (child answers, "I don't know").

"Suddenly, Billy heard the loudest sound there ever was (child shakes very loud sound). Billy was so surprised he said, 'What was that?' And he heard a voice say (child speaks) 'Don't be scared it was just Susy (child's name) making the very loudest sound!'"

Game 5: Ordering Soft, Loud, Very Loud

Six sound choices: two soft, two loud, two very loud

Observable Behaviors

The child will determine which sounds are soft, loud, and very loud, find two that are the same in each category, and place them on appropriate faces on game sheet.

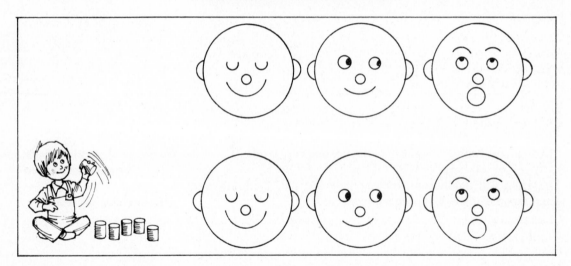

Appropriate Teacher Dialogue

Can you find the sounds that are soft? Loud? Very loud? Can you find another sound that is soft? Loud? Very loud? Place the sounds on the faces.

After the child understands procedure, leave so that the game may be played independently. Return when game is completed. Shake the containers to check the findings.

Game 6: Using Sounds Expressively

Three sound choices: soft, loud, very loud

Observable Behaviors

The child will determine which sounds are soft, loud, and very loud, place the shakers on appropriate faces, and use these shaker sounds to accompany songs.

*Find the sounds that are soft, loud, and very loud. Put them
on your game sheet in the correct places* (on faces). *Listen to
these songs. One of your sounds will make a nice accompaniment while we sing. Will you use a soft, loud, or very loud
sound for this song?*

Teacher sings *Rock-a-Bye, Baby* or another lullaby
Child chooses a soft sound to play.

Teacher sings a clackety train song.
Child chooses a very loud sound for accompaniment.

Teacher sings any nursery rhyme where medium loud is appropriate, *Hickory, Dickory, Dock* or *Humpty Dumpty*.
Child chooses a medium loud sound for accompaniment.

   Upon completion of each song, the child places the accompanying sound on the correct picture in the game sheet. Encourage the child to sing his own songs and accompany them with
the shakers.

SOUND STUDY 4:   SANDPAPER PUZZLE

Sounds may be relatively loud or soft (*volume*).
Sounds may gradually become louder or softer.

Music Concepts

Construct a puzzle board to which a sequential story strip may be
attached at the top. Manipulatable sandpaper blocks may be
placed below. Prepare six blocks: two without sandpaper, two
with fine paper, and two with coarse paper. The puzzle may be
fitted into a shallow tray.

*Setting the Learning
Environment*

Objectives of the Study   Given an opportunity to manipulate puzzle pieces using auditory clues, the four- or five-year-old child will sequentially place sounds to express an idea.

Play   The puzzle with story strips is placed in individual work area. Through dialogue and experimentation, the child learns to use the sounds to tell story of train coming from afar, drawing very close, and going away.

The child tells story by making "choo-choo-choo" rhythm with sound starter on each block, moving from left to right (just as the story does).

Other story strips can be created for use with this puzzle.

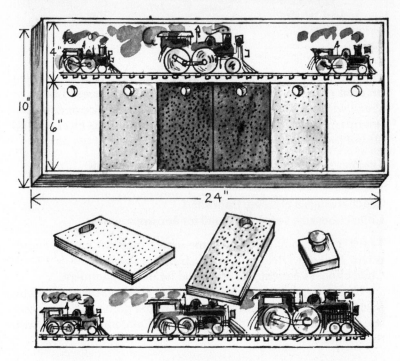

Observable Behaviors   Does the child seem to understand the concept of cause and effect necessary for sequencing activities?

Does the child select appropriate sounds to express story sequence?

Does the child use sound, visual clues, or both to determine sequence?

Appropriate Teacher Dialogue   *Can you tell me a story about this little train?* Possibly cover all but the first train with sheet of paper. Slide paper to show next part of story as child describes what is seen.

Do you think you can hear that train when it is really far away? Find a soft sound for the far-away train. How will the train sound when it comes closer (Louder)? If the child selects coarse paper block but plays it appropriately, one would accept that he had the concept of loud and soft and would consider the story well told.

Key Words are "loud and soft," "getting louder or softer," "very loud or soft."

This same game board can be used as a *tempo* (fast and slow) game. Create pictures of slow train and fast train on the story strip. The child uses any of the sandpaper block sounds, but the manner of playing should reflect faster and slower.

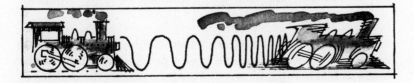

SOUND STUDY 5:   SOUND PADDLES

Sounds may be relatively high or low *(pitch)*.
Sounds have distinctive characteristics *(timbre)*.
Sounds may be relatively loud or soft *(volume)*.

Music Concepts

Create several sound paddles by purchasing flat wooden stirring spoons (rice paddles). Hammer three small box nails into the widest section and stretch rubber band around nails.
Place sound paddles in work areas, table, or soft corner. After initial experience, leave in a place accessible to children.

Setting the Environment

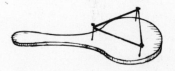

Given an opportunity to explore sounds of the instrument, the child will discover that sounds of strings may be loud or soft and high or low.

Objectives of the Study

Children freely explore the sound paddles; eventually teacher suggests first plucking the rubber band, listening for the sound it produces (soft sound), and then holding the flat side of the paddle against the ear and plucking again. The child will delight in the contrast between the two ways of playing the instrument, for in the second the child hears a rich string sound. Explore different sounds of other paddles in both playing positions. Encourage children to share the sound by holding the paddle against someone else's ear.

Play

Observable Behaviors   Does the child notice differences in sounds that the three sides of the rubber band make?

Does the child demonstrate, through gestures or comments, a realization of differences (loud or soft) when playing instrument in two positions?

Does the child use new and known music vocabulary?

Appropriate Teacher Dialogue   While pointing at rubber band:

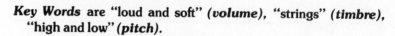

> *Play this shorter side.*
> *Play this longer side. I hear a higher sound when you play here! Lower when you play here!*

Key Words are "loud and soft" *(volume)*, "strings" *(timbre)*, "high and low" *(pitch)*.

To extend this activity for older children, prepare a mat containing outlines of several sound paddles and small boxes. Invite a child to organize a sound piece by placing the paddles on the mat with instructions for playing. The child decides the sequence for playing each sound paddle by selecting a small card that indicates H (high), M (middle), and L (low) sound to be played. The card is placed beside each paddle.

After completing the composition, the child first plays it himself and then invites someone else to play the sounds in the order indicated.

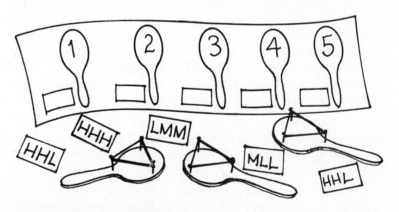

Sounds of Strings: The Miniharp   The small five-bar harp may be left in an accessible place for children to use whenever they wish. The instrument is so small that a three-year-old can easily manage to carry it. The instrument may be fitted with a braided shoulder strap so that it may be hung around the child's neck, minimizing the danger of a child's accidentally dropping it.

The young child is quite satisfied to strum at random with or without using the chord buttons.

Sounds may be relatively fast or slow *(tempo)*, long or short **Musical Concepts**
(duration), loud or soft *(dynamics)*, low or high *(pitch)*.
Sounds have distinctive characteristics and qualities *(timbre)*.

Prepare a sound wall, approximately 4 feet square, to be placed **Setting the Environment**
in the sound box.
1. Trace around various sizes of drums to be used; cut circles in
    board so that drums may be inserted.
2. Place drum wall in sound box. Provide such assorted sound
    starters as soft beaters and drum brushes.

Given an opportunity to play in the sound environment using **Objectives of the Study**
beaters and fingers on drums, the child will randomly explore
sounds that are long and short, loud and soft, fast and slow, and
high and low. The child may use these sounds to express musical
or extramusical ideas.

The child plays with sound starters that have been placed on the **Play**
floor of the sound box or may explore sounds by striking drums
with hands or beaters.

Observable Behaviors   Does the child explore using different sound starters?
Does the child seem aware of pitch differences in the drums?
Does the child use new and known music vocabulary?
Does the child demonstrate interest in sounds of drums by returning to the environment?

Teacher will probably intervene initially to supervise safety precautions. This activity involves swinging beaters; thus there is the chance of accidentally tapping another child. Major concerns for safety occur during the first few moments when children are most freely exploring sounds. Limiting the area to two children at a time and using beaters with relatively short sticks will eliminate most problems.

Appropriate Teacher   I hear Robin tapping on the drums.
Dialogue   *What a good sound, "rumpa-pum-pum!"*
Who can make a sound of a walking giant?
Who can make the sound of a little princess walking?
Who can walk slow? Faster? Begin to run?
Who can rub fingertips on drums? Can you hear a long, rubbing sound?
Who can make pitter-pat sounds with fingertips?
Can you hear those little short sounds?

Key Words are "thudding," "thumping," "fast," "slow," "loud," "soft," "long," "short," "low," "swishing," "drums," "big," "little."

Create New Interest in the   Place pictures in the same environment as motivators for sound
Drum Wall   play or sound stories:
Little boys walking and running;
Horses walking and running;
Snake crawling;
Horse running;
Long lines (long sounds);
Short lines (short sounds);
Jack and the beanstalk *(Who can be the giant? Jack?)*;
The hare and the tortoise *(Who can be the rabbit? The turtle? Who will move with a fast sound? A slow sound?)*.

More Drum Play   One or more drums can be played as a part of movement activities inside the room or outdoors. Drums can be explored at learning center tables or used to accompany songs.

Lisa and Jerry were attracted to the work table where a ten-inch hand drum, a small beater, and a pegboard game had been placed. Lisa began making sounds on the drum while Jerry created designs by laboriously sticking the multicolored pegs in the board.

The teacher joined the children. She and Lisa made the sounds of walking and running feet on the drum. The teacher turned the drum over, thumped the open edge rather than the skin head, and invited Lisa to try this new sound. Jerry, with hands full of pegs, became interested and edged toward the activity. Attempting to gain attention, he tossed several of the pegs into the inverted drum.

The teacher seized the opportunity to involve Jerry by saying, "Jerry, you have found a new way to make sounds in the drum. Did you hear those little short sounds when the pegs bounced in the drum?"

The game was on! Lisa and Jerry were rapidly gathering pegs and dropping them in the drum. "Thud, thud," went individual sounds, while loud sounds were made by whole handfuls of pegs being dropped.

The teacher emptied the drum frequently, and the game was replayed. Many comments were offered relating to the short, quick, loud, and soft sounds.

Then, a most interesting discovery was made. If one peg was

Observing Children Learn

dropped into the drum and allowed to roll around, it made a soft, continuous sound. As more pegs were added, the "roll around" sound became louder and louder.

A child-initiated, spontaneous activity turned into a most graphic way to demonstrate a basic technique used by composers: gradually louder sounds can be achieved within a composition by adding more of the same sounds.

SOUND STUDY 7:   TIMBRE MATCHING GAME

Musical Concepts   Sounds may be used to express musical or nonmusical ideas (*expressive totality*).
Sounds have distinctive characteristics and qualities *(timbre)*.

Setting the Environment   Create and place individual sound boards on a table with several wooden-headed mallets. Make two each of the following sound boards:

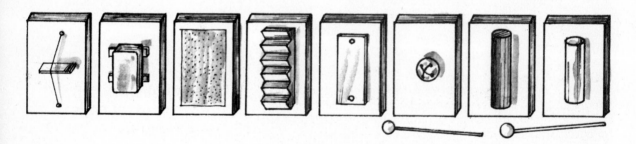

Ringing objects must move freely to produce sounds, so bells should be mounted on foam strips or tied loosely.

Play   Teacher keeps one set of sounds (control), while children are given the working set. The control set is placed in a row on the table. Teacher taps one sound and asks child to find the same sound in the working set. Child matches both visually and aurally; the teacher must be sure that the child taps both sounds to see if they are the same.

Upon repeating the game, the teacher may place the control set in lap, out of view of the child. The child then matches using only auditory clues.

An even more complex game may be played by using rhythm patterns when matching sounds. Child matches and echoes rhythm pattern of teacher:

Child finds correct sound and echoes rhythm pattern on the bell.

If sound boards are unobtainable, the same study can be undertaken using small percussion instruments from the rhythm set. Use two each of jingle clogs, jingle bells, drums, maracas, ratchet sticks, plain sticks, and sandpaper blocks.

Does the child successfully match sounds when using visual and auditory clues?
Does the child successfully match sounds by auditory clues alone?
Does the child use new and known musical vocabulary in reference to the sounds?

Observable Behaviors

Key words are "clicking," "clattering," "swishing," "thumping," "ringing," "chiming," "same," "different."

Appropriate Teacher Dialogue

SOUND STUDY 8: CHIMES

Sounds may be relatively high or low *(pitch)*; long or short *(duration)*; loud or soft *(volume)*.
Sounds have distinctive characteristics and qualities *(timbre)*.

Musical Concepts

Prepare and hang random lengths of brass or other metal tubes from the top of the sound box. Attach lower part of each tube to floor of box to prevent hazardous swinging. Provide dowel sticks for sound starters.
   The sound of chimes can become very dense in the classroom. The teacher may control this by exchanging heavier beaters for lighter, softer rubber ones or hanging chimes outdoors from a tree or play equipment.

Setting the Environment

Given an opportunity to explore, the child will assimilate ringing sounds and grow in awareness that they may be relatively long or short, high or low, and loud or soft.

Objectives of the Study

Children explore sounds in the box, using a variety of sound starters. They will quickly discover that the heavier sticks make

Play

louder sounds and that the chimes of different lengths make higher and lower sounds.

Children may use bell sounds expressively as fire truck bells, train, church chimes, or ice cream vendor's cart. Teacher may wish to add sandpaper blocks to provide additional timbre for train sounds.

Observable Behaviors Does the child explore, testing the sound of each stick on the chimes?

Does the child have coordination skills necessary to strike the narrow surface of the chimes?

Does the child use sounds expressively (sound stories) or merely enjoy random sounds?

Does the child use new and known music vocabulary?

Appropriate Teacher Dialogue Any references to musical terms reflecting concepts are appropriate. Guide the child in playing a *sound-silence game*. Strike a chime: then grip it with free hand to stop sound.

I hear sound. Now I don't hear the sound!
How long will this sound be?

Key Words are "sound" (not "noise"), "silence," "long," "short," "ringing," "chiming," "bell-like," "loud," "soft," "high," "low."

Chime Xylophone

Using a chime xylophone is a good follow-up activity after children have freely explored the larger sound study. Chime xylophones are available commercially at many toy stores. The design of the instrument is such that the tubes are placed on a foam mat; thus, individual pitches are removable. Many delightful melodies may be played by placing only the "G-E" pitches on the foam mat. As the children play these sounds, simple songs can be sung, like *Rain, Rain, Go Away* (page 75) or *Ring Around a Rosy* (add additional pitches; page 75).

Children may delight in just rearranging the tubes and playing sounds. The chimes are tuned to individual pitches within a scale. At a later time, the instrument may be used as one traditionally uses a xylophone.

SOUND STUDY 9:   RESONATOR BELLS

Musical Concepts

Sounds may be used to express musical or nonmusical ideas *(expressive totality)*.
Sounds may be relatively high or low *(pitch)*.

Setting the Environment

Create a bell wall by cutting spaces in a board and slipping resonator bells into them.

Arrange the bells from low to high by making groups of three-two-three to form the following pentatonic scale: C D E G A c'd'e'.

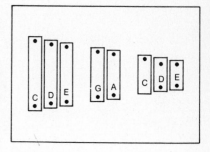

Place the bell wall in the sound box, or create a similar arrangement in another music area. If bells cannot be arranged in the "wall," they may be left in the carrying case with unused bells turned over bottom side up. The case should be turned so that the bells are in a vertical arrangement from low to high. Place a few mallets near bells.

Play

The child initially plays by freely exploring sounds of bells. No reference is made to scale arrangement.

Another day, pictures may be added that indicate ideas of

"up" and "down." Sound stories and songs like *Jack and the Beanstalk* or *Hickory, Dickory, Dock* may be used. One child tells the story by referring to characters, while another plays the sounds to help express the ideas.

Observable Behaviors   Does the child demonstrate a growing awareness of up—high and down—low?
Does the child use the sounds appropriately when telling stories?
Does the child use new and known music vocabulary as part of the play?

Appropriate Teacher Dialogue   Sound stories may result from the children's ideas. Going up in the sky in a jet or rocket or the fireman climbing the ladder are most useful story openers. The teacher takes cues from the child's interest of the moment.
Key Words are "up—high," "down—low," "going up," "going down," "ringing."

Resonator Bell Wall

A More Difficult Bell Activity Use only specific bells. Pull out all bells except one or two, like G and E. The child may choose between these two sounds to create accompaniments for songs, for example, *Bye, Baby Bunting* (page 75).

Encourage children to create their own melodies while playing sound combinations: G E or C D E G A or G E A.

Music Motivators

A music motivator has no inherent sound. It only suggests possible musical play. The objects should have some elements of manipulation in order to hold the child's interest. Such motivators might be puzzles, puppets or pictures that are topically involved in music.

THE MUSICIANS

Cut musicians and their instruments from cardboard or wood. If using wood, drill a hole so that the instrument can be attached to the musician. A small wooden peg is fastened to the bass viol, guitar, and bass drum (Tinker-toy assembly method).

The child manipulates the puzzles, joining instruments to musicians. Teacher provides vocabulary:

piano	*guitar*	*bass drum*	*trumpet*
boom-boom	*ta-ta-ta-ta*	*zing-zing*	*musician*
bass viol	*strum*	*parade*	

Children sing the sounds of the instruments and incorporate musical terms in their conversation.

Teacher may at this time display pictures of musicians playing instruments in the area and play recordings of these instruments (piano, trumpet, drums, strings).

MAKE-BELIEVE RECORD PLAYER

1. Prepare a box with two small holes in the top.

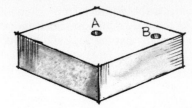

2. Create a wooden turntable to be inserted in hole A; leave small space between turntable and box to allow spinning motion.

3. Make record player arm of wood. Place the peg in hole B. The arm should freely swing over but not touch record.

4. Records are made of tagboard or masonite, black with white label.

   Arm, turntable, and records are removable so child can assemble the puzzle as well as play the music-making game.

Observing Children Learn When the children arrived one rainy morning, they saw a new item on the table in the music center, the make-believe record player. They were drawn to it by the color and many puzzle pieces.

The teacher joined two of the children who were busily exploring the pieces.

Teacher "Raymond, what do you think this can be?"
Raymond "I don't know."
Teacher "Susie, have you ever seen anything like this before?"
Susie "You're s'posed to put this here." (Susie twisted and clattered the flat discs until she placed one on the center post of the turntable).

Teacher "Susie, I think you're right. You know, this is a make-believe record player and these are make-believe records. This record player makes imaginary music. You can choose any record you want, and if you sing for it you will hear the nicest music. Would you like to try one?"
Raymond "I can put this one on."
Teacher "Good, Raymond. What song will this be?"
Raymond (No answer.)
Teacher (thinking of the day's weather) "Could it be about a boy in the rain?"
Raymond "Yes."
Teacher "O.K., here it goes. Put the needle on the record."
(Teacher begins to model a song:
"There was a little boy; he was singing in the rain. He sang about rain drops . . drip-drop . . . drip-drop.") "What else could he sing about? Could he sing about rain splashes?"
Susie (Clutching a record) "He could sing about mud puddles."
Teacher (singing) "He could sing about mud puddles."
Susie "Sing about rain drops."
Teacher (singing) "Sing about rain drops."
Raymond (singing) ". . and cars and boys."
Teacher (echoing Raymond's pitches) "And cars and boys."
Susie (impatient to play her record, sings) "And that's all!"
Teacher (singing) "And that's all!"
Teacher "That was a pretty good song. Who can find another?"
Susie "I can, I can. Mine's about a cookie monster."

The game continued with others joining the group. The children sang known and improvised songs. Each was anxious to have a turn to use the record player.

Playing Pitched Instruments

Xylophones

One of the most useful instruments in the early-childhood music experience is a small xylophone with removable wooden or metal bars. The teacher can control the pitch responses of the child by removing sounds that are not needed. The flexibility of this instrument over the traditional xylophone design is important; it enables the child to perform successfully because tonal responses have been placed within certain limitations.

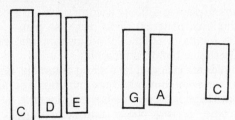

These xylophones usually have a range of an octave or more. They include the diatonic scale from C to c'. Orff-type instruments have additional F♯ and B♭ bars that allow children to play in the keys of G and F as well as in the key of C.

These xylophones can be used for improvised melody-making, composed melodies, ostinati, and other harmonic accompaniments.

Xylophone Experiences with Three-Year-Olds

An early experience using this instrument with Threes might be as follows:

Teacher places the xylophone, preset with limited bars (pentatonic scale), and a hard mallet on the floor.

The child uses the xylophone; the teacher uses a recorder or another xylophone.

1. **Child explores sounds, taking bars off and on, looking, touching, and hearing.**
2. **Child strikes the instrument, sometimes very hard, other times rather sensitively.**
3. **Teacher allows free play for the first moments, then joins in by playing the recorder. The teacher uses only tones of the pentatonic scale when making up melodies.**
4. **The teacher does not attempt to match the pitches that the child is playing but does follow the child's beat and tempo. If the child plays fast, teacher does, too. The teacher must respond very quickly to the child's changes.**
5. **At first the child may seem to pay little attention to the sounds of the recorder. After only a brief time, it becomes obvious that there is much awareness of and even careful listening to the sounds of both instruments.**
6. **The child becomes aware that he is controlling what happens and is delighted with the sudden possession of power.**
7. **Often the child will stop, and of course the teacher instantly stops, too. The game has now turned into a sound-and-silence game.**

During one such session, the child suddenly stopped. There was a long silence. The teacher said, "I think you're trying to trick me!" This only rekindled the child's enthusiasm for the game.

Playing Pitched Instruments in Relation to Other Instruments

Tape an ensemble playing ostinato accompaniments (short, repeated melodic or rhythmic patterns). You may use piano, guitar, other classroom instruments, or ask the school instrumental teacher to tape sounds of orchestral or band instruments.

Two examples are included for a string ensemble. Record each of these patterns for approximately three minutes. The first pattern is very smooth and legato; the second is short, staccato.

Place the tape, cassette player, and xylophone in the learning area. The pitches shown below each pattern may be used to perform improvised melodies on the xylophone.

The teacher will observe interesting responses as the patterns change. The child tends to reflect the change from smooth to staccato in the method of articulating the melody.

Ostinato Patterns for Strings

Scale for Improvisation   Arranged by Glenn Fifield

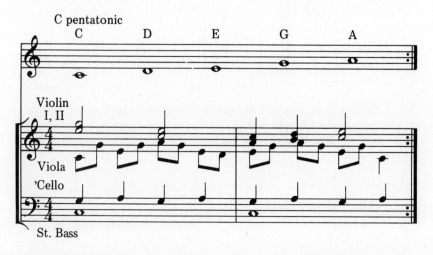

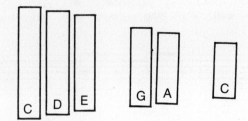

Bar Instruments (child's pitches)

Scale for Improvisation

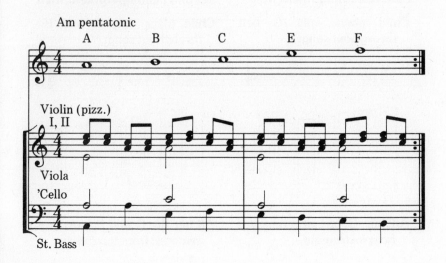

Bar Instruments (child's pitches)

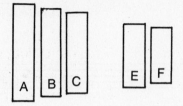

Exploring sounds of instruments evolves into performing simple melodies and accompaniments. An accompaniment can be as simple as one or two sounds. All bars except the pitches needed are removed.

Ding Dong Bell

Traditional Nursery Rhyme

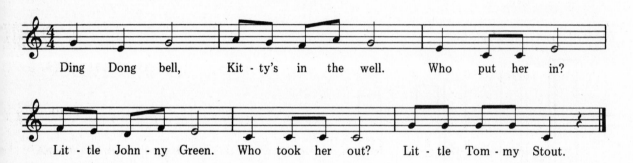

Ding   Dong   bell,   Kit - ty's   in   the   well.   Who   put   her   in?

Lit - tle   John - ny   Green.   Who   took   her   out?   Lit - tle   Tom - my   Stout.

First accompaniment idea

Child plays only G bell throughout song:

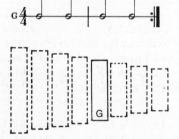

All but G bar are removed from instrument.

Second accompaniment idea

Child plays only G and E throughout song:

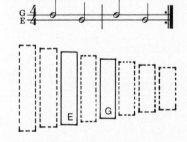

All but the G and E bars are removed from instrument.

As children grow in ability to do several things at one time, they can be expected to sing, dance, and play instruments simultaneously.

The following arrangement can be used in a variety of ways. It includes singing, chanting, expressively moving, and playing instruments both rhythmically and melodically.

The teacher may use parts or all of these suggestions, depending on what the children are capable of performing.

Skiddle Dive

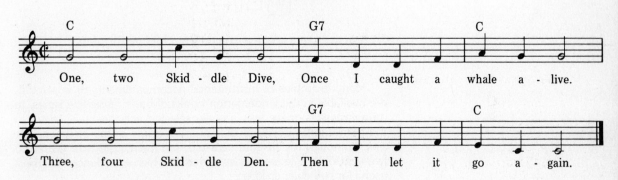

One, two Skid - dle Dive, Once I caught a whale a - live.

Three, four Skid - dle Den. Then I let it go a - gain.

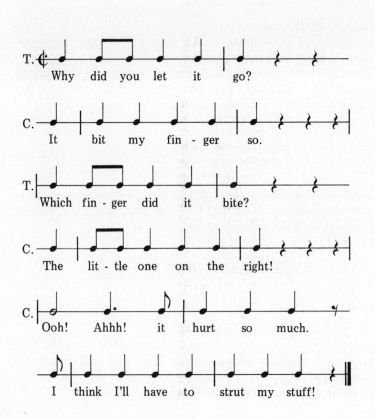

T. Why did you let it go?

C. It bit my fin - ger so.

T. Which fin - ger did it bite?

C. The lit - tle one on the right!

C. Ooh! Ahhh! it hurt so much.

I think I'll have to strut my stuff!

Child chooses a percussion instrument—jingle bells, triangle, drum, maracas, or claves—to play while dancing.

Another child makes up a melody for the dancer using these pitches on a xylophone:

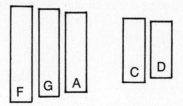

Repeat song and chant with another child performing.

Many examples of instrumental accompaniments or ensembles are available in the kindergarten books of basic music text series. In most instances, these are carefully selected activities, well suited to the performance ability of the children. Some of the selections are simple enough for the four-year-old, but mainly they are geared to five-year-olds. The teacher must decide which experiences are most useful for particular children.

1. Old MacDonald

The child sings the familiar melody (key of F). Begin singing on pitch of A. Place bells in vertical order as shown.

First invite the child to play the C bell repeatedly throughout the song. The child may play with the rhythm pattern of the words or in relation to the basic beat (one to one or two to one).

Another time, invite the child to play "G" accompaniment except when singing "E-I-E-I-O." At this time bells E D C should accompany the descending melodic idea.

2. Little Jack Horner—Little Miss Muffet

Introduce the bell accompaniment by clapping hands on the first beat of each measure while singing. Then add bell sounds by playing from the lowest to the highest sound on the first beat of each measure. The sequence repeats for phrase two.

Little Jack Horner—Little Miss Muffet

1. Lit-tle Jack Hor-ner Sat in a cor-ner, Eat-ing a Christ-mas pie;— He
2. Lit-tle Miss Muf-fet Sat on a tuf-fet, Eat-ing her curds and whey;— A

put in his thumb, And pulled out a plum, And said, "What a good boy am I!"—
long came a spi-der And sat down be-side her, And fright-ened Miss Muf-fet a - way.—

3. Whosery Here?
Sing the song. Use the children's names and sing about the color
clothing they are wearing. Accompany the song by playing the
bells with the basic beat. The child may choose any combination
of bell pitches and make up repeated harmonic patterns.

How many different ways can you accompany this song?

Children may also use jingle clog, tambourine, ratchet sticks, jingle bells, wood block, or maracas.

1. Who's been here since I've been gone? Pret - ty lit - tle girl with a
2. Who's been here since I've been gone? Good look - ing boy with a

red dress on. Whos - er - y here and been - er - y gone?
plaid shirt on. Whos - er - y here and been - er - y gone?

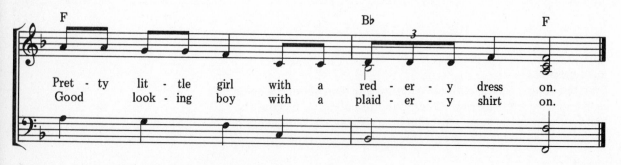

Pret - ty lit - tle girl with a red - er - y dress on.
Good look - ing boy with a plaid - er - y shirt on.

There is music in the country . . .

rustling trees,

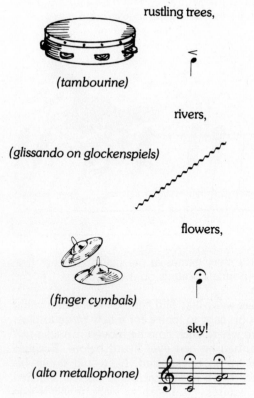

(tambourine)

rivers,

(glissando on glockenspiels)

flowers,

(finger cymbals)

sky!

(alto metallophone)

And those who listen, hear it in their hearts.

(drum)

Keyboard

A piano is available in most preschool classrooms. Often it is thought of as the accompaniment instrument available only for the teacher's use. On the contrary, children should be allowed, even encouraged, to explore the many sounds of this instrument:

high – low	harp sounds	smooth – disconnected
loud – soft	keyboard sounds	long – short
fast – slow		

Teachers often overstructure the initial experiences by attempting to teach the child to play melodies by writing numbers on the keys or using color codes. Playing melodies on the piano requires many coordination skills and mature musical understanding of rhythm and melody. The child may too easily become frustrated or uninterested when subjected to this approach.

There are more appropriate child-centered activities to be experienced by the young child at the keyboard. The following are a few suggestions upon which the creative teacher may expand.

KEYBOARD STORIES

Teacher and child play story games at the piano. Teacher first tells the story making appropriate sounds on the keyboard.

Once upon a time there was a little bird named Pete. Being rather bored, he flew out of his cage to look a for a new place to play. He landed on a place where each time he moved, his little feet made higher sounds than he had ever heard before. Because these high sounds were so unexpected, he would flutter his wings, then settle back down again. Each time his feet touched down, he heard the sounds. He began to walk, trying to see where the sound was coming from. He stepped here and here (down keyboard).

Meanwhile, a rather large cat named Thomasina also discovered a new place to sleep, and much to her surprise she discovered that each time she moved her paw or stretched her claws a low and unusual sound was created.

Thomasina began to stretch and move. Pete continued to step, step, step! Pete's sounds became lower and lower; Thomasina's sounds became higher and higher! (The cat and bird began to move to the center where they meet, and of course, the cat chases the bird right back up and over the keyboard.)

Who would like to be the cat Thomasina? Who would like to be the bird Pete?

Create story "scores" by cutting strips of tagboard as long as the piano keyboard. Sketch story ideas typical of the examples above. Place the strips on the keyboard for the child's use when performing.

Can you make your fingers go up just as the little boy is walking?

You and a friend make your fingers walk up just as the children are walking.

Use sounds to make a rainstorm.

The frog and bird sing to each other.

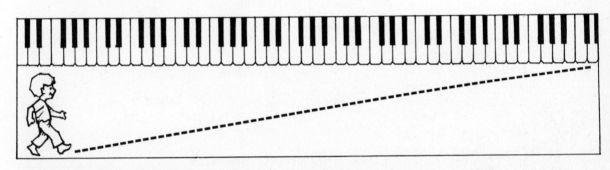

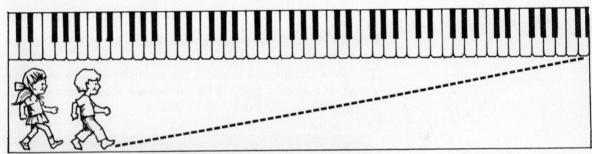

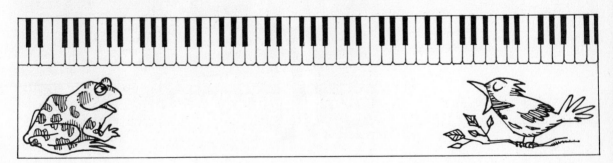

EXPLORE WHITE KEYS

Use one finger. Can your finger begin down low and play each sound (white keys) to the very highest one?

Can you make each finger play its own sound? Just use four fingers of each hand.

Choose from

high   middle
low

long 〜〜〜   short 〜

loud   soft

Sleepy music

Wake up music

LONG AND SHORT SOUNDS

One child plays any sound on the keyboard by touching and quickly removing fingers.

The second child tries to catch the sound by playing the "hold pedal" at bottom of piano. If he catches the sound, he may make it long or short, whichever he chooses.

SHARED IMPROVISATION _____

Teacher and child or two children may create improvised music as suggested here.

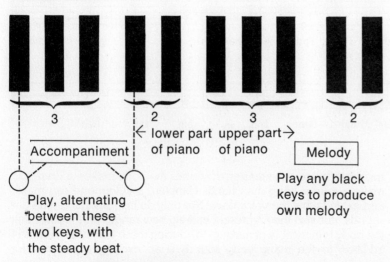

Accompaniment

← lower part of piano   upper part → of piano

Melody

Play, alternating between these two keys, with the steady beat.

Play any black keys to produce own melody

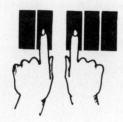

Use pointer fingers of each hand to play accompaniment or move up and down for melody.

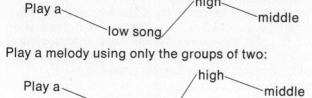

Play a melody using only the groups of three:

Play a — low song — high — middle

Play a melody using only the groups of two:

Play a — low melody — high — middle

PLAYING A FAMILIAR MELODY

Use only two sounds.

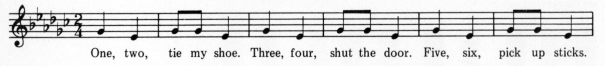

One, two, tie my shoe. Three, four, shut the door. Five, six, pick up sticks.

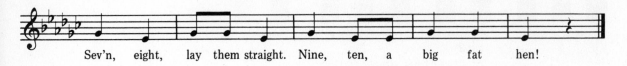

Sev'n, eight, lay them straight. Nine, ten, a big fat hen!

Summary Instruments are an extension of sounds the body makes: a drum can make a louder bang than hands clapping; a xylophone can match and extend what the voice does. Not only do instruments extend our sounds, but also they represent entirely new ranges and timbres that the body is incapable of making. Producing these delightful sounds in addition to the many body sounds is an exciting experience for children.

Children begin dealing with sounds by becoming aware of their existence, then exploring in a number of ways:

1. Manipulating sound-making objects;
2. Imitating heard sounds;
3. Discriminating between sounds;
4. Classifying sounds;
5. Ordering sounds;
6. Improvising with instruments;
7. Organizing sounds to communicate ideas and feelings.

There are countless methods for using instruments as a part of the music experience. There are many ideas in texts and other supplemental material, and new suggestions may be obtained at music workshops.

The teacher should be a collector and creator of classroom objects that represent valid sounds. A sound is valid and meaningful if it fulfills the purpose for which it is intended. That is to say, a pie tin will make a clinking sound but will not have the ringing sound of a brass cymbal. The pie tin may be useful in a timbre identification game involving same and different sounds, but is less useful as a makeshift cymbal to accompany a song.

When collecting sounds for use in the classroom, determine the learning objective and then find the best quality sound (musical or environmental) to meet this need. Within each collection, fine musical instruments should be included. The very young child must experience beautiful sounds in order to grow in valuing music.

The activities suggested in this chapter have used the following sound sources:

sandpaper
sandpaper blocks
assorted mallets and sound starters
brass tubes
sound cylinders
chime xylophone
rice paddle/rubber bands
five-bar Autoharp
assorted drums
drum brushes
pegs
hand drums
jingle bells

jingle clogs
maracas
sticks, plain and ratchet
triangles
finger cymbals
resonator bells
Orff-type xylophone
Orff-type metallophones
soprano recorders
tambourines
piano
cassette tape recorders

Why We Do 6
What We Do

Planners of any curriculum must recognize how the child receives, stores, recalls, and uses understandings at various stages of development. Material to be learned must be arranged in sequence and made available to the child in the most appropriate manner at the most appropriate time. Only through such an approach can the most effective programs be planned.

Educators responsible for teaching music in early childhood have often developed programs by relying on intuition coupled with their own musical background and observations of children. The attitude, often valid, has been, "I feel this is good for children, but I'm not sure why!" At our best, we have leaned heavily on observing responses and initiating subsequent activities, logically building upon the child's newly acquired musical understandings. At our worst, we have tended to perpetuate methods based on the way we ourselves were taught and on random samplings of individual experiences teachers had found successful. The result has often promoted play experiences rather than **learning** through play. Music educators seeking more reasoned directions for curriculum choices must consider theories proposed by psychologists working in the areas of learning and child growth and development.

Routes to cognitive development for the young child have been investigated carefully by the eminent theorist Jean Piaget. Others whose work has influenced early education are Jerome Bruner and Maria Montessori. The findings of these theorists have resulted in new methods and materials in all curricular areas. Though their theories have been disseminated for several years, they demand continued study and application if we are to improve our curricular goals and objectives. Also, more recent research in the psychology of consciousness may provide yet other perspectives on how the child thinks and develops.

The following material will briefly summarize the theories of Jean Piaget, Jerome Bruner, and Maria Montessori. Of these individuals, Maria Montessori alone has specifically developed a music curriculum for children. We shall also touch on recent approaches to brain research.

Included in each of these studies are comments relating the theories to music education. With the exception of the Montessori material, these comments have been prepared by the author. They are intended to help the reader realize why we do what we do when preparing music experiences for young children.

Piaget: Cognitive Development

Piaget's theory of cognitive development has significantly affected early childhood curriculum planning by providing insight into the thought processes of the learner. The following material represents a brief summary of some of Piaget's thinking. Implications for music have been projected as interpretation of the child's thought process as related to music and are not specifically part of Piaget's original study.

ASSIMILATION	ACCOMMODATION
• newly perceived data.	• processes perceived data forming "schemes."
• enables quantitative expansion, not change.	• enables qualitative expansion and change.

EQUILIBRIUM

Equilibrium occurs when there is a balance of assimilation and accommodation. The learner strives to maintain this balance.

Disequilibrium occurs when there is an imbalance of assimilation and accommodation. The learner seeks balance to further assimilate and accommodate.

Piaget stated basic assumptions about the way children learn.

1. The child does not think like an adult.
2. The child learns by becoming involved with concrete objects.
3. The child learns intrinsically (from within) not extrinsically (from without).
4. The child evolves intellectually through the generative nature of the prior experience and the quality of the current experience.
5. The child learns through the adaptation of new schemas (formation of concepts; categorizing perceived data).
6. The child uses two interdependent activities, assimilation and accommodation, in this adaptive process. Assimilation is the taking in of perceptual data; accommodation is a modification in the way of thinking to accommodate perceived data.
7. The child strives to establish equilibrium when assimilating and accommodating new data.

Growth in the cognitive area is seen as a sequence of qualitative changes of schemas logically forming from prior categories. New schemas are incorporated; they do not replace prior ones.

Stages of Cognitive Development

Piaget divides intellectual development into four stages. The stages are hierarchical and involve a maturation process; thus characteristics of prior stages are not entirely displaced by new stages. Children develop intellectually in the same manner but not necessarily at the same ages.

Sensorimotor—up to 2 years
Preoperational—2 to 7 years
Concrete operations—7 to 11 years
Formal operations—11 to 15 years

Concrete operations and formal operations will not be discussed here since they are beyond our immediate concern.

Sensorimotor Period

This is the prelanguage period. The infant utilizes senses and motor reflexes to begin building an image of the world. The child at this time is egocentric, sees the world only from his own point of view, is unaware that other points of view exist. During this stage the child learns by acting on the environment.

Preoperational Period

This stage is characterized by the development of language and rapid conceptual growth. The child moves from functioning largely with concrete objects to symbolic representation (words).

Piaget states that intelligence appears well before language. It is based on the manipulation of objects; in place of words and concepts, it uses perceptions and movements organized into action schemes.

Sensormotor Period

Begins to orient self to

objects

space

time

Causality

learns about cause and effect

Object Permanency—

objects can exist without being seen

Intentional Behavior

initiates goal-
directed activities

Preoperational Period

Egocentric Speech
tends to think actions
out loud—has conversations
with self in presence
of others

Socialized Speech
deliberate exchange
of ideas

Piaget believes sensorimotor operations are the basis for language development. The young child can understand language and express ideas through actions long before being able to verbalize understandings.

The two- to four-year-old works very hard to acquire language, and language accelerates the rate at which experiences can take place. According to Piaget, the child moves through two stages in using language, the egocentric and the socialized.

Characteristics of the preoperational stage that prevent the child from attaining completely logical or mature, adult-like thought are egocentrism, centering, transformation, and irreversibility.

"Egocentrism" expresses the child's inability to see any point of view other than his own, the belief in the correctness of his own thoughts, and the belief that everyone thinks in the same manner. The child does not deliberately strive to be egocentric but is unaware that there could be alternative ways of thinking.

"Centering" describes the child's way of fixing attention on a single perceptual feature at a time. The child is unable to process information from other aspects of the object.

Transformation, the ability to integrate a series of events from beginning to end, eludes the very young child. The child's attention focuses on each element in the sequence rather than on how they transform from one state to another.

Children in the preoperational stage lack the ability to reverse thought, that is, they cannot reason back to the point of origin of a thought or event.

Problems of conservation also derive from the inability to reverse thought. Conservation is the awareness that the amount or quantity of an object remains constant even though that object may change in shape or position.

IMPLICATIONS FOR MUSIC

Centering

A cassette tape recorder was used as a sound source. The child centered on the on/off buttons. Music was perceived only as something to control, not as something to hear. Attempts to redirect attention to the music were ignored by the child. The child's awareness was centered on the button that controlled sound and silence.

Transformation

From a musical standpoint, the study is designed to explore concepts dealing with dynamic changes; sound can express an idea by gradually becoming louder.

There are many concepts confronting the child in this particular study: big − little, near − far, and soft − loud.

Sound study

Soft and loud sounds are produced by using sandpaper textures. Child uses sounds to express idea of train coming from afar to very close.

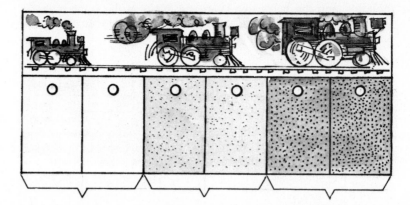

Child thinks	This is a little soft train.	This is a big loud train.	This is a very big loud train.
Child does not think	This is the little train. It is far away and very soft.	This is the same train coming closer, getting louder.	This is the same train, very close and loud.

Five-year-olds begin to demonstrate the ability to perform this particular task.

Irreversibility

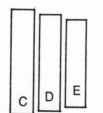

    The child asked to play the notes in this order repeatedly must be able to reason back to where the pattern started. In the early stages, the child is not likely to do this.

Conservation

The following music conservation task was conducted by M.L. Serafine.[1]

The child listens to steady clicks, is asked if the clicks are getting faster, slower or remaining the same. The child answers, "The same." The clicks are again presented, this time sounded with rhythm patterns superimposed. Again, the child is asked if the clicks are faster, slower, or the same.
The child answers either "faster" or "slower," not conserving that the clicks are still the same.

Reliable music conservation-type studies analogous to Piaget's are more difficult to construct in that the child's limited language becomes a factor. The question is raised as to whether the child is unable to conserve or language is getting in the way of expressing what is heard.

The ability to reverse thought or to conserve is gradually developed through the cognitive and sensorimotor actions of the child. Piaget believes conservation cannot be directly taught but is acquired by the child through experience.

Cognitive development of the child moves steadily along during the preoperational stage. The process of assimilating and accommodating proceeds by initial and continual acts as the child refines schemas by the following:

Discriminating;
Categorizing;
Ordering;
Improvising.

Near the end of this stage, the child begins to demonstrate some rather sophisticated mental processes:

Recalling;
Reordering;
Conceptualizing.

Beginning of abstract thought are activated in this stage. The child moves from dealing almost exclusively with concrete objects to using symbols (language) and concepts in a most effective manner. Consequently, this period in the child's total development is most significant.

Bruner: Theory of Instruction

Jerome Bruner has contributed much to a rationale for curriculum development. In *Toward a Theory of Instruction,* he has merged what is known about intellectual growth with theories of instruction. Since each of these domains is complex in its own right, he concludes that the issues to be faced extend beyond what we have formally recognized as matters of education or child rearing: "We are dealing with the subject of how culture is transmitted . . . and how in transmission, it produces more effective and zestful human beings."[2] The following material briefly outlines Bruner's view of intellectual growth and his theory of instruction. Implications for music have been added.

1. Growth is characterized by increasing independence of response from the immediate nature of the stimulus.
2. Growth depends upon internalizing events into storage systems that correspond to the environment.
3. Intellectual growth involves an increasing capacity to say to oneself and others, by means of words or symbols, what one has done or what one will do.
4. Intellectual development depends upon a systematic and contingent interaction between a tutor and a learner.
5. Teaching is vastly facilitated by the medium of language, since language is the medium through which the learner can bring order into the environment.
6. Intellectual development is marked by increasing capacity to deal with several alternatives simultaneously.

Bruner has stated that there are three ways by which human beings translate experiences into a model of the world and that they are used in sequential stages.

1. Enactive stage—action: The child knows many things for which there are no imagery-words; thus, we cannot teach using only picture diagrams.

IMPLICATIONS FOR MUSIC

The child must move, do, sense, play,

and act upon his environment.

2. Iconic stage—imaging: The second system depends upon visual or other sensory organization and upon summarizing images. This is a stage of internalization: the individual can retain the image when it is no longer present. An **icon** is the instructional device to help the child internalize.

[2]Bruner, Jerome, *Toward a Theory of Instruction,* Harvard University Press, © 1971, p. 149.

We may infer that for a child to internalize an image in music, the icon must be as nearly visually descriptive of the sound as possible.

An image of long and short or a melodic contour would look like this:

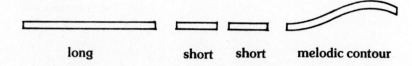

| long | short | short | melodic contour |

3. Symbolic stage—representation: At this stage communication of thought takes place through language and visual systems; certain images and words stand for an idea or object.

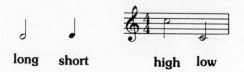

| long | short | | high | low |

In Bruner's view, man's progress depends upon his ability to use tools, instruments, or technologies that help him to express and amplify his powers. Unless basic skills are mastered, later and more elaborate skills become increasingly inaccessible. According to Bruner, "One 'teaches' readiness or provides opportunity for its nurture; one does not simply wait for it."[3]

Bruner's theory of instruction is principally concerned with how to arrange environments to optimize learning. He has suggested that curriculum planners follow these guidelines:

1. Specify the experiences that effectively create interest in learning.
2. Specify ways in which knowledge can be most readily grasped by the learner.
3. Use effective sequences.
4. Specify nature and pacing of rewards and punishments.
5. Shift from extrinsic reward, teacher praise, to intrinsic reward, pupil achievement.

Bruner has concluded that almost all children possess intrinsic motives for learning and do not need rewards lying outside the activity they impel. Such motives include curiosity, the drive to achieve competence, admiration of competence models (someone whose respect the learner wants, standards the learner wishes to adopt), and reciprocity, the deep human need to respond to others and to operate with them toward an objective.

From Bruner's work, implications for music in early childhood can be drawn. "Readiness" for the young child indicates an acting, sensing, doing interaction with music which transfers to imagery and

[3]Bruner, *op. cit;* p. 29.

iconic representation of the sounds and finally evolves to the more accurate and effective means of communicating understandings through symbols.

When able to utilize the shortcuts of symbolization, the child becomes more powerful in controlling and expressing musical ideas. Throughout these stages, the child must operate from an intrinsic need to know. The curriculum must be built so that the child will value what is learned.

Montessori: Self-education

Maria Montessori, a physician and noted biologist, became interested in the learning process through working with mentally retarded children; her theories and methods are based on observation. She was greatly concerned that children progress as a result of interacting with objects and ideas within the classroom. She stated, "The secret of all man's progress is the love of his environment."[4]

One of the strengths of her program lies in its power to motivate learning through self-teaching and corrective materials. Montessori set forth several principles in relation to the educative process:

1. Children are not miniature adults but are in a stage of continuous and intense change.
2. Children cannot be educated by other people; they self-educate, freely choosing from materials designed to instruct.
3. The teacher's role should be primarily that of observer, intervening as necessary, setting environment to encourage the spirit of inquiry.
4. Methods are based on practical life experiences. Children are actors in a living scene.
5. Methods are designed not so much to give new impressions as to give order to impressions already received.
6. Children's goals must be respected. The doing of the act may in itself be the aim. Children are not necessarily product-oriented.

Montessori evolved a curriculum for all phases of learning with music as an integral part of the program. With colleague Anna Marie Maccheroni, she created specially designed sound sources and didactic materials (materials designed to instruct) for the children's use.

Montessori and Maccheroni devised a program that included music theory and ear training by having children participate in varied activities:

1. Playing instruments;
2. "Auditioning" (listening to music);
3. Moving expressively;
4. Singing.

In this program, materials are placed in the environment, and children are led by their own curiosity to use them. Such skills as auditory discrimination, tonal memory, and the ability to order and classify sounds are all part of the developmental process.

Bells, sound cylinders, dummy keyboards, visual rhythmic materials, staff boards, discs, notes: all are part of Montessori materials to be used by the children. A few of these materials have specialized design and use, as described in the following section.

Mushroom Bells

Mushroom bells are individual sounding bells shaped like small mushrooms. The bells form the equivalent of two sets of the chromatic scale.

One set of mushroom bells can be ordered according to scale by using visual and auditory clues. As these bells become higher in pitch, they decrease in size. The bell bases are painted black and white, correlating with the keys of the piano. This set is identified as the Control Bells in sound-matching games.

The second set contains only auditory clues; thus, it may be ordered only by listening and determining which sounds are relatively higher or lower. These bells, mounted on brown bases, are called the working bells.

The following musical games are described in *Developing the Senses,* by Anna Marie Maccheroni.[5] The student wishing to investigate the Montessori approach will do well to seek out this material.

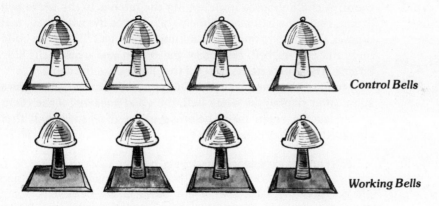

Control Bells

Working Bells

PROBLEM-SOLVING GAMES FOR MUSHROOM BELLS

1. A little child plays with one bell, transfixed by a single sound. The child may handle the bell in varied ways:

a. Playing it repeatedly;
b. Holding it nearby or faraway;
c. Listening to vibrations;
d. Listening to the sound soften to silence;
e. Playing the bell on edge or middle;
f. Exploring the appearance of the bell.

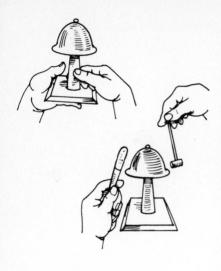

2. The child learns to carry the bell with one hand on the stem and the other under the base. The child explores sounds of the bell by using mallet and damper and may discover that the best quality is produced by striking the bell on the edge, using the mallet in pendulum movement.

The child can make long and short sounds, controlling duration by touching the bell with the damper. Alternatively, it is possible to play a sound and match it by humming or singing.

3. To play a matching game, give a number of children each a white bell and another equal number of children a brown bell. Initially use two or three random pitches; then increase the complexity of the game until children are working with the eight pitches of the major scale.

A child with a brown bell finds the child who has the matching sound in the white bell. The two children with the same pitch stand together and play their bells; the teacher hears that the pairing is correct.

4. Play a tonal memory game. Begin with a limited number of different pitches; then increase to eight.

Place white bells in a given area and brown bells across the room. A child chooses from among the pitches in the white bell group, rings this bell many times, then leaves the white bell, and crosses the room to find the matching brown bell. When the child finds the correct bell, he places the brown and white bells side by side. The child checks to see if the pitches are the same.

Increase the complexity of the game by increasing memory span. After ringing the white bell, the child goes out of the room or circles the room twice before seeking the brown bell that sounds the pitch originally played.

After many experiences matching bells at random, the child is ready to organize sounds on the board. The board has white and black spaces the same size as the bases of the bells. The board provides a model for the tonal relationships of the major scale in that the half steps between three and four and between seven and eight are spatially closer together.

The white bells are used as controls and are placed at the rear edge of the board; the brown bells are the working bells.

PROBLEM-SOLVING ACTIVITY

Place one white bell in the appropriate spot near the rear edge of board. Two brown bells are used, one matching the tone of the white, the other different. The child explores sounds, matches the same sounding white and brown bell.

Extend the game by placing all eight white bells on the board. Use only one brown bell. The child must find the one with which it pairs and place it in front of the same sound.

Although the mushroom bells have a very resonant sound, they are useful to children for performing melodies. Children should be encouraged to make up their own tunes and also to play tunes of others. The bells should be used as musical instruments, not merely as sound studies.

Bar Bells

Individual bar bells, typical of the resonator bell, are also available for the child's use. These bells may be manipulated on a board that has spaces marking the various intervals of the scale. The child can organize the bells chromatically, then use them as a keyboard instrument to perform melodies.

Sound Cylinders

Cylinders containing such various materials as salt, rice, or corn are placed in the environment. The cylinders are of wood, allowing no visual clue as to content. The child must rely solely on hearing to match and order sounds. Double sets of cylinders containing the same sounds are used. The child plays with the cylinders to determine same and different and to order sounds from softest to loudest.

Other Manipulative Materials

Moving from the sound-making devices, the Montessori materials deal with more abstract symbols representing music. Association is made between sounds and the musical symbols on the staff.

A staff board with places for discs representing note heads is available. The discs relate information on syllables (do, re, mi), numbers, or colors (black or white), and may indicate durational value of the note head. The child works with both the treble and bass clef, dealing with higher and lower sounds. Such games are played as writing or singing or playing the child's name on each step of the scale. After writing on the scale, the child is encouraged to play from an original score, using any of the bell-type instruments or piano.

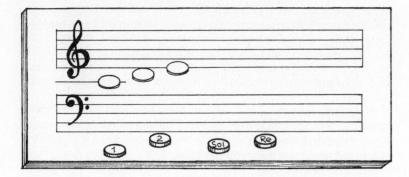

The didactic materials include several types of staff and manuscript music paper for permanently notating compositions.

Rhythm is approached through wooden rods of varying lengths. Abstract music symbols are printed on white rods; brown ones are used as spacers.

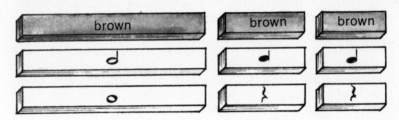

Montessori used the term "hooking" to mean the linking of one experience to the other. It is crucial to the child's growth that each experience be purposeful and that it lead to another of greater challenge. The child, though freely choosing, works within the scope and sequence of instructional materials.

The Montessori approach to music education of very young children takes direct advantage of the sequences of childhood learning. Many of the materials and methods are useful. In some instances, they tend to move the child rather quickly into written responses involving the theory and fundamentals of music. Using didactic materials to include additional sound sources and problem-solving experiences is most valuable to an early childhood music program.

The Learning Process

There is much activity at the present time by scientists and psychologists in brain research, activity in which the educator has also a professional interest; evolving theories bear directly on the instructional process. Triggering the keen interest of educators has been the discovery that the two hemispheres of the brain have special functions. Serious questions have arisen as to whether or not we are involving both hemispheres in our approach to education.

Study of hemispheric functions is only one among several areas of brain research that significantly relate to how the individual learns. Educators are also reviewing data on such other matters as how the brain deals with perceptual information, memory storage, and arousal motivation (attending). Educators find themselves reviewing the anatomy of the brain and other parts of the central nervous system, acquiring new vocabulary in order to understand scientific research.

Questions raised in a few areas of study are listed here to apprise the reader of topics that hold promise for future curriculum directions. A detailed bibliography (page 193) is provided for those who wish to pursue any of these topics further.

Memory

Learning implies a change in behavior as a result of experiences; further, it implies storage of the results. The brain has an infinite capacity for memory. Memory can be short-term or long-term. Perinent questions in this area of research are these:

1. How is the brain altered for information storage?
2. How does the function of long- or short-term memory affect the educational process?

Attention

Attending is the ability to fix on a specific object or idea, screening others out. The intensity of the fixation and its duration are a part of the process of attending. The ability to concentrate long enough to process information is crucial to learning.

Scientists are studying how the brain is aroused and measuring the intensity of its activation. In this activation, brain rhythms and small electrical events occurring on the cortex are measured through the use of electroencephalograms. During testing, the movement of the pupil of the eye further indicates attention response. These questions are asked:

1. When one attends to a more difficult task, does the level of activation increase proportionately?
2. Can the individual be trained to recognize loss of attention, thus controlling this action?

Perception

Perception can be tracked early in the development of the organism. How and when the child sees, hears, touches, smells, and tastes have all been reported in detail.

Educators are familiar with much of the research on visual and auditory functions, for these have been crucial to reading and language development. How one responds with motor control has also been carefully considered in curriculum development, but we have not achieved the peak of knowledge in these areas. New research continues to provide insight as to which area of the brain receives and processes sensory information. Knowledge of the neural pathways along which the input and output travel becomes important, for the malfunction or interruption of these paths cause learning disabilities.

Music therapists have probably dealt better with these concerns than have most music educators. They have developed certain activities for remediation of learning disabilities based on understanding the detailed functioning of the brain.

Hemispheric Dominance

Why has it become increasingly important for us to know which area of the brain receives and processes certain signals? Current research has indicated that the brain consists of not one but two functioning masses. The left and right hemispheres each control specific mental activities that affect the conscious state of the individual.

The left hemisphere has been found to deal specifically with analytical, logical thinking. It is highly verbal (language) and deals with events in time, like sequence and cause and effect.

The right hemisphere is more holistic, intuitive when processing information. It is nonverbal, time-independent, and deals with space orientation, artistic endeavors, and certain aspects of music.

The left hemisphere controls the right side of the body; the right hemisphere controls the left. Thus, output systems cross in the body.

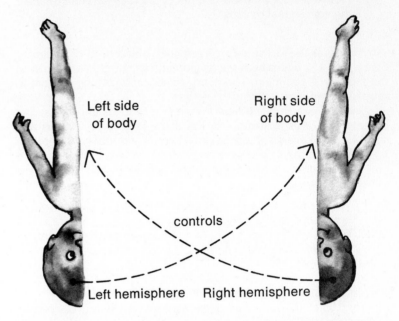

Left side of body   Right side of body

controls

Left hemisphere   Right hemisphere

It is important to view the functions of each hemisphere as dominant but not necessarily exclusive of one another (the right hemisphere does have some verbal skills).

The traditional education system has focused on teaching students to think logically, to analyze and develop language facility. The question is now raised whether we have neglected one half of the individual's growth potential.

1. Have we been so keen on developing modes of thinking through verbal skills that we have underestimated the learning that occurs through the nonverbal approach?
2. Do we allow for hemispheric superiority in individuals? Can some people be better at dealing with problems through visual-spatial rather than verbal perception?
3. When and how much more effective is the learning process when both hemispheres of the brain are functioning interrelatedly?

One significant outcome of these investigations may be that we can no longer view the nonverbal areas of the curriculum as mere enrichment. We may well find that they are as important to the student's ability to solve complex problems as are the language skills.

Understanding how the child processes information has always been **Summary** important to the person developing curriculum. Awareness of the research in such other fields as psychology, neurology, and psycholinguistics may provide new insights applicable to music education. The music educator must look beyond his own field to search out answers. There may be a whole new set of questions to be asked as to how the child learns.

Evaluation 7

Program evaluation must be a daily process. How a child reacts to one experience determines what the next should be; learning must lead to more learning. As the children have limited verbal skills, we must base much of our evaluation on what we see them doing.

There are many behaviors to observe:

1. Approach tendencies—willingness to participate;
2. Perceptual skills—sensory responses;
3. Conceptual development—thinking skills;
4. Physical abilities—vocal range, motor coordination.

Each of these areas is evaluated in relation to a given developmental stage and to its effect on the musicianship of the child.

Gathering data as to the effectiveness of a program or a child's individual progress can be approached in several ways. The tools for evaluation suggested here have in no way been standardized but represent only a few ways to obtain feedback. The materials rely heavily on the observation method of accumulating information.

The following materials are presented as guides or yardsticks. The items will not be applicable to every child.

Observable Musical Behaviors

In general, three-year-olds will exhibit these characteristics:

Growing awareness of differences in sounds (environmental and musical);

Growing ability to locate sounds in space;

Curiosity about the many different timbres of musical sounds (clicking, ringing, thudding);

Increasing musical vocabulary;

Limited ability to classify and organize sounds in groups (one-to-one basis);

Ability to *see* and hear similarities and differences in sounds;

Growing ability to hear similarities and differences in sounds without visual clues;

Growing ability to use voice inflection to produce own melodies and portions of composed songs;

Deliberate choice as to entering group action song activity; tendency to listen, follow movement instructions with only occasional songmaking;

Beginning use of music in the company of other individuals, not necessarily aware of sharing;

Movement from random mechanical improvisations (playing) to awareness of interacting with other musical stimuli;

Growth from reflexive use of "sound starters" (sticks or mallets) to more controlled action;

Response with some regularity to own feeling of basic beat;

Movement to music or verbal suggestion that does not involve a great deal of imagery or conceptual thinking:

"Move *like a* butterfly . . . bee . . . frog . . . (not so effective)

"I see Randy's scarf move up and down,
Sometimes it nearly touches the ground!" (more directly related to the child's experience of the moment).

What other musical behaviors have you observed in threes?

The four-year-old shows development in these behaviors:

Greater ability to share and work in various size groups;

Greater ability to sustain interest in musical task at hand;

Continued playing of random pitches on instruments; however, more knowing interaction with other musical accompaniment;

Growth in ability to see and hear sound relationships; enjoyment of games involving simple tonal and timbral discrimination tasks;

Growth in ability to sequence simple ideas and use sounds expressively;

Demonstration of a feeling for phrase in improvisations (vocal and instrumental);

Liking for nonsense, silly language, and rhyming songs and chants;

More sensitive response as a member of instrumental or vocal duets (improvisation);

Ability to sing specific tones of song more in tune when beginning on own choice of pitch;

Growing ability to match tones of others;

Growing ability to respond to tonal center when vocally improvising with instrumental accompaniment;

Greater vocal participation in action song experiences;

Increasing use of musical sounds as a part of play environment;

Increased rhythmic accuracy in chanting and singing.

What other musical behaviors have you observed in fours?

Five-year-olds have usually progressed to a stage at which these characteristics may be expected:

Greater ability to cope with group activities;

Increased use of imagery in expressive movement and improvised song lyrics;

More sophisticated use of improvisation that involves organizing, recall, and reorganizing skills;

More effective handling of sequence (cause and effect), as in sound stories and other organizations of sound;

Growing ability to reverse a trend of thought; ability to remember and play simple repeated patterns;

Greater capability of movement that requires 1) increased sense of balance; 2) feeling of steady beat, and 3) repeated movement patterns;

Increased rhythmic accuracy in chanting or clapping basic beat and rhythm pattern of words;

Increased skill in matching tones of others;

Growing tonal and rhythmic memory;

Ability to meet simple "inner-hearing" challenges;

Awareness of multiple sounds played simultaneously;

Ability to improvise with a feeling of phrase;

Greater ability to respond appropriately to such differences in sound as tempo changes; sustained or detached, long or short, loud or soft, and high or low tones;

Growing degree of tonal and rhythmic accuracy when singing composed songs appropriate to ability level.

What other musical behaviors have you observed in fives?

Children come to school with some musical behaviors. They undoubtedly perform more freely and skillfully at home with parents than at school. Therefore, it is useful to enlist the aid of the parent to determine how the child is already using music. A request for parental assistance might take the following form:

Assessing Musical Growth

Dear Parent:

How does your child use music?

Please assist us by completing the enclosed questionnaire. When answering, remember that musical behaviors are not only performance skills like singing and moving to music. Awareness and curiosity about sounds are also important indicators of your child's musical interest.

The following checklist encompasses a wide span of behaviors, some beyond the normal ability of the three-year-old. Many of the skills mentioned are those we will be dealing with in the preschool.

Which, if any, of these skills have you already observed in your child at home?

Child's Name _____ Age _____ Years _____ Months

Observed Musical Activity	Frequency		
	Often	Occasionally	Rarely
Does your child . . . move to music (on television, radio, record player, performed in the home)? —seem to move rhythmically with a feeling of basic beat? —enjoy freely moving? —enjoy moving to finger-play and song games?			

	Often	Occasionally	Rarely
. . . sing to self or with others?			
—make up own rambling tunes (naptime songs)?			
—sing simple melodies fairly accurately when singing alone?			
—sing parts or all of such melodies as Sesame Street songs, television commercials, nursery rhymes, birthday songs?			
—sing simple melodies fairly accurately when singing with others?			
—sing as a part of play ("making dolly sing")?			
. . . listen to music?			
—exhibit curiousity about sounds (environmental as well as musical)?			
—recognize differences in environmental and musical sounds?			
—enjoy toys with musical sounds?			
—request or play special recorded music?			
. . . play musical instruments?			
—explore piano keyboard using fingers?			
—play familiar melodies on keyboard or xylophone?			
—play toy piano, xylophone, drum?			
. . . play with environmental sounds?			
—find sounds in kitchenware?			
—tap rhythmically on furniture or wall?			

Musical Resources in the Home (please check):
Stereo   Radio   Piano   Television   Guitar   Other Instrument(s)

Parent Comments:

Approach Tendencies Toward Music

How willing are the children to participate in music activities? You may wish to spot check or keep a running log on how children individually or as a total group become involved in various music activities within the classroom.

These observations may be carried out at random or as detailed research. The teacher's goals will dictate how and what information is needed. Data of this kind can be particularly helpful in refining specific materials and shaping future directions.

APPROACH TENDENCIES

Learning Activity: _____

CHILD'S NAME_____
AGE_____
   (years-months)
DATE OF OBSERVATION_____

APPROXIMATE TIME SPENT IN ACTIVITY:

	2	4	6	8	10	12	14	16	18	20	22	24	26
Non Participation													
Distant Observer													
Close Observer													
Limited Participation													
Eager Participant													

NATURE OF PARTICIPATION

Evaluating the Quality of the Experience

The plan for learning is an evaluation tool. It provides immediate feedback: Did the experience accomplish what was expected?

In the past, when creating lesson plans, the teacher noted the necessary materials and role to be played during the activity. We must go one step further to be accountable for learning. We must attempt to predict what the **child** should be doing as a result of the teacher's plan of action.

A lesson plan[1] that serves as an evaluation tool needs to include this information:

1. What the teacher will do;
2. Behaviors the teacher might expect from the child;
3. The level of thinking skills with which the child will be involved;
4. Prediction of possible learnings.

In a given music experience, the child will probably be observed singing, playing (instruments), manipulating, listening, speaking, or moving.

The thinking skills fall in a range of learning levels of various complexities. For our purposes the levels can be consolidated into four categories: knowledge, analysis, synthesis, and evaluation. Each level can be described to help the teacher determine the nature of the thought processes involved. Descriptive words help the teacher identify the nature of activities within each level of learning.

Levels of Learning	Description
label name recognize describe	Knowledge
discriminate classify order compare	Analysis
improvise create perform arrange	Synthesis
choose accept reject	Evaluation

The child operates on these levels as a means to learning. The knowledge level is the lowest level of learning; evaluation and decision-making represent the highest, but the levels are interdependent in the learning process.

The young child acquires knowledge about many things and in the process is recognizing and labeling: "This is a bell, a drum." Simple analytical tasks are a part of many matching games: "These two sounds are the same; this one is different!"

The child working at the synthesis level is beginning to organize and use information, possibly creating a song knowingly or unknowingly using something heard in the environment.

To evaluate, making a choice based on information from earlier experiences, the child operates at the highest level of learning: "Don't play that! That's not a good song to put my dolly to sleep 'cause it's too loud!"

A MODEL FOR PLANNING EXPERIENCES _____

Use the following plan in this manner:

1. Check the nature of the activity. Will it be child-initiated, with free exploration? teacher-initiated, with intermittent intervention?
2. How many children will participate in the activity?
3. What materials must be readied?
4. Write what teacher will do. This may include questions to be asked or other dialogue.
5. Check word(s) in the column showing what child does.
6. Check word(s) in the column indicating the thought processes.
7. Write what the child will specifically learn as a result of the activity.

LESSON PLAN MODEL

Planning the Experience   DATE_____

NATURE OF THE ACTIVITY	CHILDREN INVOLVED AT A GIVEN TIME:_____	MATERIALS:
__Child Initiated __Free Exploration __Teacher Initiated __Teacher Intervention __Teacher Directed		

TEACHER DOES:	CHILD DOES: (Observable Behaviors)	IN ORDER TO: (Thinking Skills)	GROW IN UNDERSTANDINGS (Student Objectives)
	Sings Plays Manipulates Listens Speaks Moves	name know recognize describe demonstrate discriminate classify order compare improvise create perform arrange choose accept reject	

SAMPLE LESSON

Planning the Experience   DATE_____

NATURE OF THE ACTIVITY		CHILDREN INVOLVED AT A GIVEN TIME: 2/3	MATERIALS: Xylophone (Bars: CDE GA or resonator bells) Cassette Player & Prepared Tape
___Child Initiated ✓Teacher Initiated	✓Free Exploration ___Teacher Intervention ___Teacher Directed		

TEACHER DOES:	CHILD DOES: (Observable Behaviors)	IN ORDER TO: (Thinking Skills)	GROW IN UNDERSTANDINGS (Student Objectives)
- Place cassette tape/equipment and xylophone (CDE GA) in Learning Center. - Initiate activity by reviewing "Stop/Start" cassette information with child. - Invite child to perform melody with the taped accompaniment. - Ask children to help, take turns with friends	✓ Sings ✓ Plays ✓ Manipulates ✓ Listens Speaks Moves	name know recognize describe demonstrate discriminate classify order compare ✓improvise create perform arrange choose accept reject	a melody that involves tonal relationships to other sounds. (perform simultaneously with other sounds)

SAMPLE LESSON

Planning the Experience   DATE_____

NATURE OF THE ACTIVITY		CHILDREN INVOLVED AT A GIVEN TIME: 2 or 3	MATERIALS: 2 bells 2 sand blocks 2 wood blocks 2 drums. mallets/beaters
✓Child Initiated ___Free Exploration ___Teacher Initiated ✓Teacher Intervention ___Teacher Directed			

TEACHER DOES:	CHILD DOES: (Observable Behaviors)	IN ORDER TO: (Thinking Skills)	GROW IN UNDERSTANDINGS (Student Objectives)
Create a sound study for Learning Center: 2 bells 2 sand blocks 2 wood blocks 2 drums. Allow children to freely explore. Intervene by placing one of each sound in a row; other four in scrambled fashion. Invite children to: 1. Find the same sound; play both; place them together. 2. Play the game with another child.	Sings Plays ✓Manipulates ✓Listens Speaks Moves	✓ name know ✓ recognize describe demonstrate ✓ discriminate ✓ classify order compare improvise create perform arrange choose accept reject	accurately matching sounds using visual and auditory clues.

158 EVALUATION

Whether the tools suggested in this chapter are used or others **Summary** devised, the important thing is to be accountable for the child's learning. The teacher who views the program for accountability can plan for learning by using appropriate techniques even though not always writing down the precise lesson.

Research is not solely the province of the university community. On-site teachers can be active researchers. Who is better able to report on responses of children than those who work with them each day? The teacher is encouraged to accumulate data and then to share information, either formally or informally, with others who are shaping curriculum. There is much to be learned from children about the way they learn. The teacher is the key to this information.

The Musically Skilled Teacher 8

The teacher's role in the early childhood environment requires the modeling of certain performance skills. The more secure the teacher is in performing music, the more effective the music session will be. The teacher is continually required to acquire and refine skills, musical or others, needed in the classroom. With what depth and breadth these studies are undertaken depends on the personal goals of the individual.

The following units of study are presented to assist the teacher in developing minimal skills helpful when dealing with preschool children. It is hoped that the individual will reach out for additional assistance. The many resources for this purpose include "how to play" books, workshops, and group and private lessons.

The Guitar

The guitar may be used to accompany familiar songs and children's improvisations. With only limited playing, tuning techniques, and three or four chords, the teacher may use this instrument most effectively in the classroom.

The guitar is a six-string instrument, usually either Spanish or classical. The Spanish guitar has wire strings that produce bright, ringing sounds. The classical guitar has a softer tone quality most appropriate for use with the soft voice of the preschool child. Its nylon strings are often more comfortable for the beginning performer as they are easier on the fingertips than the wire strings of the Spanish guitar.

Learning to Play

Get acquainted with the instrument Be able to identify the following parts of the guitar.

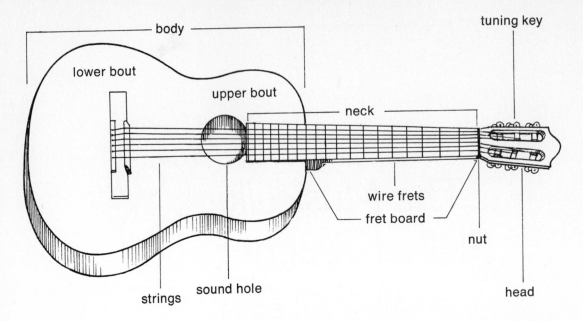

Tuning · Tuning requires skills in matching pitches. At first it is often difficult to determine whether the string to be tuned is below or above the desired pitch. Practice this skill by matching appropriate strings with pitches on piano, pitch pipe, or other strings on the instrument itself. While learning, seek assistance from the music specialist at the school or other persons able to tune the guitar.

Numbers and Pitches of the Strings

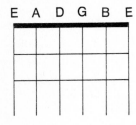

One Way to Tune

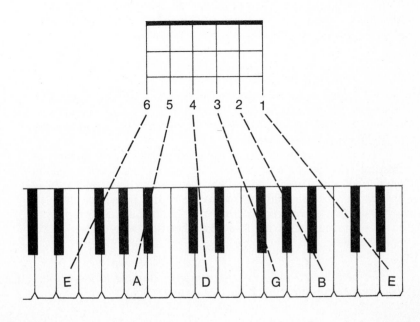

Playing Position   Keep guitar in vertical position. Do not turn it to look at strings; if necessary, lean head over to see finger changes.

Rest right arm on lower bout; place fingers in easy reach for strumming.

You can prop your foot on a size one coffee can to help hold the guitar in a proper playing position.

Left-Hand Position   Gently swing left arm at side with hand in natural, relaxed position. Bring hand up in same position. Notice how fingers are gently curled. This is the correct position for the left hand.

The guitar neck fits into the U-shape created by the thumb and middle finger. The neck never touches the palm of the hand, only fingertips. This position allows the hand and fingers to move freely, changing positions on the strings.

Fingering Positions   Placing fingers of the left hand on strings in certain frets enables one to change pitches and produce melodies or chords.

Place fingers on strings in frets slightly behind the wire; not on top or in the middle of the fret.

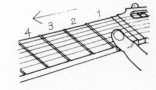

Frets are numbered:

Strum

Use right thumb and strum downward over strings.

One-chord Songs

Learn the E-minor chord. Strum with the first beat of each measure while you sing *Hey, Ho! Anybody Home?* As soon as possible, create your own strumming patterns to accompany this and songs that follow.

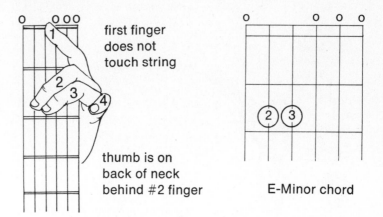

first finger
does not
touch string

thumb is on
back of neck
behind #2 finger

E-Minor chord

Hey, Ho! Anybody Home?

English Round

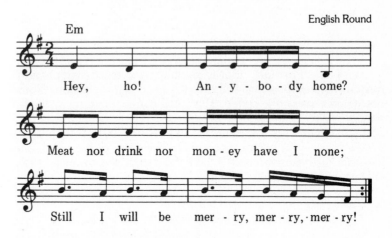

Em

Hey,   ho!   An - y - bo - dy home?

Meat   nor drink nor   mon - ey have   I   none;

Still   I   will   be   mer - ry, mer - ry, mer - ry!

Strum the E-minor chord throughout this song.

Lullaby My Jamie (Aija, Anzit, Aija)

Soothingly

Em

1. Lul - la - by   my   Jam - ie,_____   Soft - ly sleep   my   child,_____
2. Snow white lambs for   Jam - ie,_____   Ev - ery kind your   own,_____

164   *THE MUSICALLY SKILLED TEACHER*

Sis - ter rocks you gen - tly; _____ Soft her hands and mild. _____
Curl - y, bob - tailed, long - tailed, _____ When a man you've grown. _____

Learn the D-major chord.

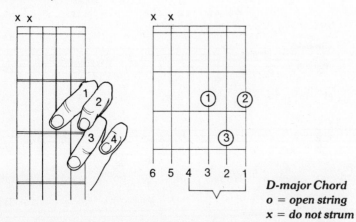

D-major Chord
o = open string
x = do not strum

When playing the D chord, you will strum only the bottom four strings (4-3-2-1). Practice strumming the chord. Press firmly on the strings to produce a full sound.

Many familiar songs may be sung using just this chord.

Song	**Beginning Pitch for Singing**
Row, Row, Row Your Boat	D
Are You Sleeping?	D
One, Two, Tie My Shoe	A
Ring Around a Rosy	A
Hot Cross Buns	F#

Two-chord Songs

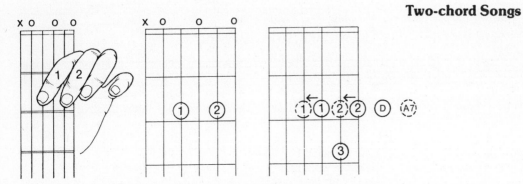

Practice moving between the D-major and A7 chord.

Sing and Strum Use this song for your own enjoyment as you learn to play the two chords. You will find that it is not in a suitable range for preschoolers to sing.

Upward Trail

Words and music traditional

We're on the up - ward trail, We're on the up - ward trail,

Sing - ing, sing - ing, ev - ery - bo - dy sing - ing, as we go.

We're on the up - ward trail, We're on the up - ward trail,

Sing - ing, sing - ing, ev - ery - bo - dy sing - ing, home - ward bound.

Here is another song for **your** enjoyment while you learn.

Down in the Valley

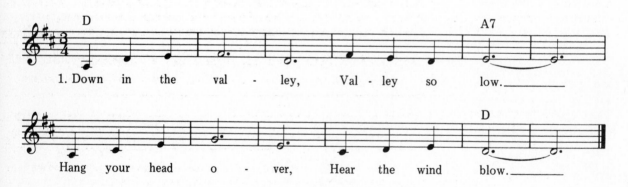

1. Down in the val - ley, Val - ley so low._____

Hang your head o - ver, Hear the wind blow._____

2. Hear the wind blow, love
Hear the wind blow.
Hang your head o-ver
Hear the wind blow.

Return to these two songs later. Use these two chords to perform them in a higher register.

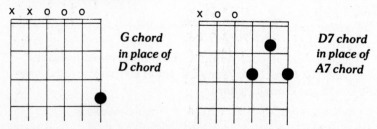

G chord
in place of
D chord

D7 chord
in place of
A7 chord

The beginning pitch for *Upward Trail* is G, for *Down in the Valley* is D.

After learning the D major and A7 chords, play them as an accompaniment as the children sing:

Mary Had a Little Lamb
Beginning pitch for singing: F#

    Mary had a little lamb, little lamb, little lamb.
    Mary had a little lamb, its fleece was white as snow.

Skip to My Lou
Beginning pitch for singing: F#

    Skip, skip, skip to my Lou,
    Skip, skip, skip to my Lou,
    Skip, skip, skip to my Lou,
    Skip to my Lou, my darling.

    Verse Little red wagon painted blue . . .

Adapting the Guitar

Children can strum the guitar for one-chord songs if the teacher adapts the instrument in special ways.

1. Retune the strings of the guitar so that a major chord automatically sounds:

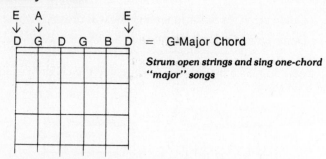

E A   E
↓ ↓   ↓
D G D G B D = G-Major Chord

Strum open strings and sing one-chord "major" songs

2. Create a *chord helper* bar for the guitar. Cut a small piece of wood as illustrated. The bar touches only the edge of neck and depresses only the A and D strings.

Glue felt onto the surface that touches the instrument. Use a rubber band to attach the bar to the instrument in the second fret.

The guitar can now be strummed by child or teacher to sound the E-minor chord.

Have a child play the guitar accompaniment while others sing *Down Came A Lady*. Tune the guitar so that the open strings will sound the G-major chord.

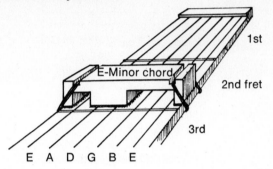

Down Came A Lady

American folksong

Change "Ol' Dan'l's wife" as follows:

Down came Ms Susie Jones and she was dressed in blue.

Down came Ol' Eddie Brown and he was dressed in blue.

Learn to play a new chord. Accompany the children as they sing this train song.

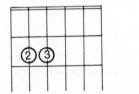
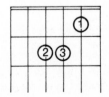

Chicka-hanka

Words and music traditional

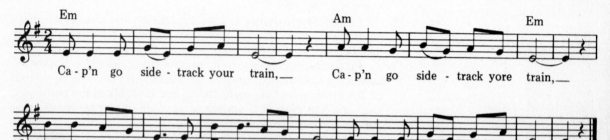

Ca - p'n go side - track your train,___ Ca- p'n go side - track yore train,___

Num - ber three in line, A - com in'- in on time, Ca- p'n go side - track yore train.___

Many songs found in the basic music texts have the chords marked over the score. Use the textbook as a source of songs to be accompanied by the guitar. Page 00 in the Appendix provides information as to additional diagrams of chords that may be needed to perform these songs.

The Autoharp

The Autoharp is a most useful instrument for accompanying songs and an excellent sound source for exploration experiences. The teacher will find it easy to play, for the instrument is designed to produce the appropriate chord automatically when a bar is depressed and the strings are strummed. The performer need only follow the letter names that indicate chords and push the corresponding button on the instrument.

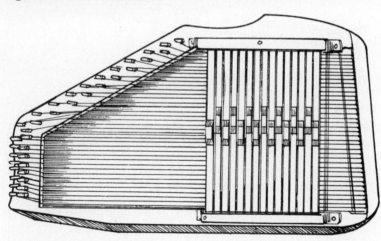

For most simple two- and three-chord songs, only three fingers of the left hand are used to press the chord bars.

The performer does not need to look at the bars once the hand is positioned. This enables the eyes to remain on the music, following written chord indications, words, and song notations. In the following

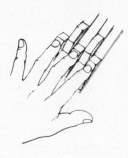

illustration of the left hand, the I-Chord is under the index finger, the V7 Chord under the middle finger and the IV Chord is under the ring finger.

The right hand usually crosses over the left and strums away from the body (from low to high strings). A variety of strumming patterns may be used.

Autoharps are available in several sizes: five-bar (5 chords), twelve-bar (12 chords), and fifteen-bar (15 chords). The more bars on the instruments, the more chords are available to the performer; thus one can play in a variety of keys or use more complicated chordal accompaniments with songs.

The small five-bar harp is a useful size for the young child. The larger harps are more effective for the teachers' use.

The Recorder

The recorder is a wind instrument that has been used in various cultures from ancient times to the present. It has a soft flutelike sound much like the voice quality of the young child. Thus, it is a good model of sound in the early-childhood classroom.

There are several ranges of recorders. The one most widely used is the soprano recorder (Baroque fingering). The following information will assist the learner in producing the most desirable tone quality and correct pitches.

right hand finger holes

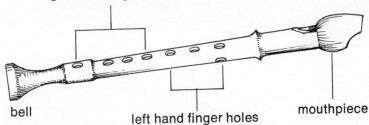

bell

left hand finger holes

mouthpiece

Learning to Play

Playing Positions

Sit straight, elbows slightly away from body, in relaxed position. Keep chin up when playing; do not look down at instrument.

Place tip of recorder mouthpiece on lower lip; cover with upper. Mouth remains in slightly smiling position.

Use lefthand fingers to cover holes of the top section. Place left thumb on single hole under the recorder; the next three fingers cover the top three holes. The holes of the recorder are covered with soft pads of the fingers, not the tips. The little finger does not cover any hole.

Use the right hand to support the instrument initially by gently gripping the bell; later, the fingers of right hand cover holes.

Producing Sound

Blow gently into the instrument. It requires very little air to produce a sound, even less air when lower tones are played. Begin the sound by shaping, but not speaking, the word "duh." Stop the sound by forming a "d" motion with tongue, thus quickly cutting off the flow of air.

Using the Recorder

It is possible to use the recorder in the classroom even if the performer has relatively few music-reading skills. The instrument may be used as a pitched sound source to create improvisations that enhance the children's music-making and understandings.

The teacher can use the recorder in these ways:

1. As a part of a game

   "I can play a high sound for Joe. . . ."
   "I can play a low sound for Sue. . . ."

2. To play familiar melodies for children

Ma - ry had a lit - tle lamb . . .

3. To create a melody while children play other instruments

Child strums the E-minor chord on guitar.	→	Teacher chooses from certain pitches to improvise a melody (E F# G A B).

Improvising means "making-up" or "creating" on the spot. The music probably cannot be duplicated and is usually not notated for others to play. Improvising can be a very sophisticated act or a simple one.

For improvising with a pitched instrument, certain guidelines will help increase the quality of the melody. These suggestions are to be viewed as starter ideas, not the only way to improvise music.

1. Work within a feeling of tonality; begin and end on a prearranged pitch.
2. Use a certain pitch set (scale) in relation to other sounds played simultaneously.
3. Work with a feeling for phrase, usually equal lengths of breath.
4. Plan to repeat some of the melodic or rhythmic patterns.
5. Use such musical controls as tempo, dynamics, and articulation of sound.

While working with improvisational ideas, gradually learn the pitches and positions on the recorder. It is not necessary to learn the entire scale at one time. Each activity is repeated many times with children, so there is ample opportunity to become proficient before going on to a new set of pitches.

IMPROVISATIONAL ACTIVITIES

THE CHILD IS:	THE TEACHER WILL:
randomly playing these pitches on a xylophone.	choose from: A C′ D′ 1. Use rhythm to vary the melody due to limitations of pitches. 2. use the pitches to follow the child's tempo changes. (faster/ slower).
strumming the G-Major Chord on the guitar. (see special tuning information)	choose from: B A G Begin and end on G to establish a feeling of tonality.
randomly playing on these pitches on a xylopohne.	choose from: A G E (may also use c′ and d′)

THE CHILD IS:	THE TEACHER WILL:
strumming the E-minor chord on guitar.	choose from: 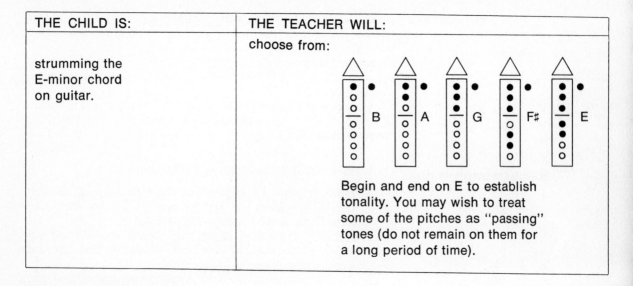 Begin and end on E to establish tonality. You may wish to treat some of the pitches as "passing" tones (do not remain on them for a long period of time).

The Most Useful Pitches to Know

Associate pitches with their placement on the staff

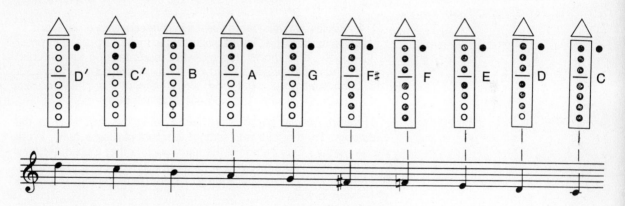

The ability to play recorder by reading from music notation opens up a wide variety of music to the teacher. The teacher may play familiar songs to help children hear melodies or accompany their movements, give pitches for songs to be sung unaccompanied, and learn unfamiliar songs by first playing them on recorder.

Playing from notation is a complex skill. Many recorder method books carefully guide the student in sequentially understanding rhythmic and melodic relationships, meter, and other symbols used in music writing. The student is encouraged to continue studying the recorder by becoming involved in one of these methods or receiving other guidance.

The recorder is a beautiful-sounding instrument that goes beyond classroom use. It provides a lovely and satisfying way for adults to express themselves musically.

Vocal Improvisation

Vocal improvising evokes very personal feelings. The performer tends to be extremely self-critical, for if the performance is seen as poor, there is no one to blame but the creator. If one were improvising on an instrument, it could be blamed for any mishaps. But the voice is **you.** It reflects one's innermost thoughts and has its own unique tone quality.

The single greatest impediment to improvising a song is the lack of self-confidence. When the teacher can move beyond this mental block, melodies flow freely.

Steps to Improvising

The teacher should try these aids to improvisation:

1. Freely explore by improvising short melodies at random. Limit self-criticism as much as possible. Do not expect first attempts to be the most musically satisfying.
2. Melodies often flow easier than words. Prepare self with words to fit possible classroom situations. Use nonsense words when others fail to come.
3. As melodies begin to take more shape, use simple pitch patterns; repeat ideas.

4. Review rhyming words useful in given classroom situations.
5. Remember that, in this instance, the main purpose of improvisation is to model and motivate music-making for the child. Thus, the melodies need not be sophisticated. They need to be similar to what one would expect the child to offer (sometimes rambling, sometimes structured).

Practice vocally improvising before using the technique in the classroom. Try the following settings in a role-playing activity. Work with a partner. One person is the teacher, the other a child. Rethink how the child would respond in given situations: verbal, nonverbal, interested but not communicating, eagerly participating, responses not always logical.

How does the teacher use vocal improvisation in such a setting? How will singing questions facilitate responses?

Frequently change roles with your partner as you move through the skill-building activities.

IMPROVISATIONAL SKILL BUILDING #1 _____

Purpose To involve child in singsong experience as an outgrowth of reading and play activities.

Role Playing Work in pairs—teacher/child.

Materials Appropriate story book.

Reading time in the "soft corner." Book shelf with many attractive books easily accessible for child. — *Setting*

Marc chooses his favorite book of the moment and brings it to teacher who is sitting in the reading corner. Two other children gravitate to the area to hear the story. Marc snuggles as close as he can to teacher and the book, eagerly searching the page with his eyes. Teacher begins to read the story but changes and focuses attention on the pictures. She asks questions about things the children see on the pages. Questions are posed in a singsong manner. — *The Experience*

Teacher	**Marc**
Do you see a kitty cat?	*"Yes," or maybe no sound at all.*
What is that (pointing)?	*"A doggie. . . ."*

EVALUATION (briefly discuss following with your partner):
1. Discuss strengths, weakness of teacher's improvisations.
2. How did the child respond?

No interest; left group — remained silently in group — nonverbal participation (actions) — occasional words — occasional words with voice inflection — many words — many words with voice inflection — singing

---

IMPROVISATIONAL SKILL BUILDING #2

To involve child in singsong experience as a part of play activity. — *Purpose*

Work in pairs—teacher/child. — *Role Playing*

Actual vessels or pantomime use of items. — *Materials*

The water table. Floating in the water are such plastic items as margarine dishes, sand buckets, small shovels, and a teapot. — *Setting*

Brian and Margie are quietly playing at the water table. They are fully involved in filling vessels with water, either using a smaller dish to fill larger ones or laboriously spooning water with small shovels. — *The Experience*

Teacher joins the play **Brian and Margie**
(Evaluate as before)

IMPROVISATIONAL SKILL BUILDING #3

Purpose To involve child in a rhythmic experience as an outgrowth of play activity.

Role Playing Teacher and child

Materials Clay or pantomime using materials.

Setting A small group of children are pounding clay and cutting it with popsicle sticks.

The Experience José is aggressively pounding his clay while talking excitedly to no one in particular. After the clay is shaped, he tosses it into the air, then roughly tears it apart. He takes great delight in piling the clay pieces precariously, directs challenging eyes at the teacher as his pieces slowly begin to topple to the floor.

Teacher joins the play   **José**

(Evaluate as before)

IMPROVISATIONAL SKILL BUILDING #4

Purpose To involve child in singsong experiences as an outgrowth of play activity.

Role Playing Father or mother and child

Materials Magazines.

Setting "Reading" time. One child and one adult.

The Experience Father or mother is sitting on couch reading magazine. Unaware of his imitation, Robby picks up a different magazine and joins parent. He climbs onto the couch, dragging the magazine, which has now opened with pages flopping. The unwieldy magazine is very much in the way of the climber. Upon successfully surmounting the obstacles, Robbie gets on the couch with the magazine more or less intact. He then begins a scooting action toward parent, sitting as close as possible. With legs outstretched, he begins to manipulate the magazine into reading position. The magazine finally ends up in a position similar to the parent's, and Robbie begins to survey the pages studiously. The fact that the magazine is upside down has not deterred his interest. Parent puts down magazine, places arm around Robby, suggests they turn the magazine right side up, then . . .

Teacher   **Robbie**

(Evaluate as before)

IMPROVISATIONAL SKILL BUILDING #5

To involve child in an echo-play song experience as an outgrowth of play activity. Teacher improvises, including rhyming words and using following pitches: G A ___ o o ___
E ___o___

Purpose

Teacher and child.

Role Playing

None.

Materials

Outdoor play. Swing area.

Setting

Brenda is attracted to an empty swing. After much wiggling and pulling, she manages to climb onto the swing seat. She then sits patiently waiting for the swing to go.
The teacher notices Brenda. "Brenda, would you like help to make the swing go?" Brenda nods yes. Teacher pushes the swing, then begins to explain how Brenda must help by straightening out her legs when the swing goes forward and bringing them back when it comes back. Brenda nonrhythmically attempts the action, meeting with little success. Teacher continues to push the swing gently.

The Experience

| **Teacher** | **Brenda** |

(Evaluate as before)

IMPROVISATIONAL SKILL BUILDING #6

To involve the child in creating songs that contain a feeling of phrase.

Purpose

Teacher and child.

Role Playing

Pantomime objects.

Materials

Teacher improvises, including rhyming words at end of sentences (phrases). Teacher encourages child to echo or make up last words of sentences. (Use following lists for possible choices; think of others that would also be appropriate)

Setting

1. *Playing with Cars*

Words in play	Rhyming Words						
Truck	buck	luck	woodchuck	Donald Duck			
Fast	last	past	overcast	blast			
Slow	doe	crow	below	calico	dough	Mexico	row
	show	throw	tiptoe	ago	bow	snow	so
	to-and-fro	undergo	low				

Varoom	zoom	bloom	gloom	room	broom	groom	whom
	assume						
Gas	glass	surpass	pass	class			
Motor	floater	toter	rotor	boater	voter		
Car	far	star	jar	Zanzibar			

2. Jumping on Rubber-tire Trampoline

Words in play	Rhyming words							
Up	cup	pup	sup					
Down	crown	frown	gown	brown	clown	town		
High	why	sign	my	tie	fly	spy	cry	eye	reply
	shy	lullaby	July	goodbye	fry	deny	buy	pie
Low	(See **Slow** under **1**.)							
Bounce	pounce	announce	flounce	ounce	jounce			

3. Rock Baby to Sleep

Words in play	Rhyming words							
Sleep	Bo-peep	cheap	sweep	creep	deep	heap	leap
	sheep	weep	keep				
Soft	aloft	coughed	oft				
Rock	clock	sock	frock	lock			
Back	black	track	lack	Mac	sack	jack	snack	stack
	crack	cul-de-sac					
Forth	north						

4. Sandbox

Words in play	Rhyming words						
Sand	band	land	hand	stand	strand	canned
Pail	tail	sail	nail	whale	bail	rail	trail	snail
	Gail						
Spoon	moon	tune	soon	prune	June		
Swish	fish	dish	wish				

5. Clay Play

Words in play	Rhyming words						
Clay	Chevrolet	pay	day	way	sleigh	pray	neigh
	hay	gray	spray	stay	they	play	
Pound	frowned	drowned	around	mound	sound	hound
	found	ground	merry-go-round				
Cut	but	rut	nut	mutt	hut		
Hit	bit	sit	mitt	fit	grit	lit	wit	slit	commit
Roll	hole	troll	bowl	pole	foal	stole	toll	casserole
	coal	maypole	oriole	patrol			
Snake	rake	ache	wake	break	cake	fake	make
	snowflake	take	mistake				

| Poke | joke folk soak choke cloak smoke broke woke |

6. *Water Table*

Words in play	Rhyming words
Float	boat wrote coat note tote goat
Spill	chill dill daffodil fill pill sill thrill hill will whippoorwill still
Splash	crash mash stash lash mustache hash
Bubble	trouble double
Slop	plop drop mop top flop cop lollipop stop shop hop chop
Drip	dip flip skip lip ship nip rip sip tip whip slip grip trip gyp
Soak	(See **Poke** under **5**.)
Wet	set debt jet met net pet yet bassinet threat sweat forget marionette gazette clarinet cigarette castanet

7. *Colored Articles (pegs, puzzle pieces, pictures, miscellaneous objects)*

Words in play	Rhyming words
Red	head sled spread lead thread wed read fed
Green	between bean jean kerosene magazine fifteen clean queen screen seen
Blue	boo zoo clue canoe do flu two shoe grew glue who through
Yellow	cello fellow bellow Punchinello
Black	(See **Back** under **3**.)
Brown	(See **Down** under **2**.)
White	night kite sight fright light bright might height right bite dynamite quite
Pink	clink sink ink wink think slink blink drink bobolink

8. *Numbers*

Words in play	Rhyming words
One	begun run bun son ton won done shun
Two	(See **Blue** under **7**.)
Three	flea see me agree chickadee dungaree tree glee he knee we free
Four	snore more door floor ichthyosaur
Five	hive alive strive dive thrive
Six	picks kicks clicks tricks fiddlesticks bricks licks ticks mix fix
Seven	eleven heaven
Eight	wait crate gate late skate
Nine	line spine shine twine divine
Ten	again then pen when wren hen men

9. *Toys*

Words in play	Rhyming words					
Bear	wear	tear	hair	stare	fair	chair	mare
Blocks	socks	box	ox	fox			
Drum	plum	some	gum	chum	hum		

10. *Movements*

Words in play	Rhyming words					
Jump	bump	thump	dump			
Run	(See **One** under **8**.)					
Skip	(See **Drip** under **6**.)					
Walk	talk	chalk	balk			
Sway	(See **Clay** under **5**.)					
Swing	ring	ding	bring	thing	string	
Slide	hide	wide	side	ride	bide	bride
Wiggle	giggle	jiggle	wriggle			

11. *Direction*

Words in play	Rhyming words						
High Low Up Down Back	(See these words under **2**.)						
Forth	(See these words under **3**.)						
Behind	mind	lined	dined	signed			
Front	stunt	hunt	grunt				
In	pin	win	begin	chin	shin	skin	tin	twin
	spin						
Out	shout	sprout	pout	doubt	scout		
Around	(See **Pound** under **5**.)						
Between	(See **Green** under **7**.)						

Other Performance Skills in the Classroom

The teacher who sings or plays piano, ukulele, or any of the other orchestral or social instruments should take every opportunity to perform for the children. Plan classroom concerts. Use music of all styles, all periods, and various cultures. Introduce children to such minimal concert courtesies as applauding and appropriate listening. (Do not perform long selections if expecting a Three to be attentive throughout.)

Summary

This unit has discussed minimal performance skills in a few areas of music-making with no attempt to cover the many instruments that are useful in the classroom. The teacher is urged to learn more about instruments like the ukulele, Orff Instrumentarium, and piano and to perform as a creator of music as much as possible.

Musical performance skills are acquired over a period of time. They require training both of muscles and of mind. One cannot become a musician overnight. As adults we tend to be impatient with our beginning attempts. We compare our efforts to those of others who may have spent many years achieving their performance level. The teacher who wants music in the classroom must be self-confident as well as willing and should not hesitate to seek assistance from qualified persons. Sensible goals and repeated practice will enable the teacher to share performance skills with the children, enriching all concerned.

Conclusion

The art of teaching is not static. One does not arrive at a point of "now I know how." When we elect to become a part of this profession, we commit ourselves to a continual search for a greater understanding of how learning comes about, how it is processed, and how we may most effectively expedite it.

The teacher who works daily with the young child is not a passive bystander but is at the core of educational change. Many fine books may be written about education, but the magic is in bringing the proposed philosophy and activities alive. Crucial to the process is the teacher's capacity to envision change, courage to try new ways, and most importantly, ability to judge effectiveness.

The child's time is precious. It must not be wasted or spent in meaningless trivia. The early years are not a time of readiness to learn; they are a time of vital active learning. The child should be offered experiences that lead to a holistic approach to learning. Musical experiences can be a driving force in total learning; The challenge to use the most effective means is before the teacher of young children.

Appendix

Resource List

Movement

Books

Cherry, C., *Creative Movement for the Developing Child*, 2d ed. Belmont, CA: Fearon-Pitman Publishers, 1971.

Findlay, E., *Rhythm and Movement*. Evanston, IL: Summy-Birchard Company, 1971

Records

1. *Creative Play*

Palmer, H., *Creative Movement and Rhythmic Expression*. Baldwin, NY: Educational Activities, Inc.

Listen, Move and Dance, Vol. I and II. Capitol Records.

2. *Imaginative Listening and Dramatization**

Selection	Composer
Ballet of the Unhatched Chicks from "Pictures at an Exhibition"	Moussorgsky (moo-SORG-skee)
Bydlo from "Pictures at an Exhibition"	Moussorgsky (moo-SORG-skee)
Dance of the Mosquito	Liadov (lee-AH-duf)
Fairies and Giants from "Wand of Youth Suite No. I"	Elgar (El-gar)
Flight of the Bumblebee	Rimsky-Korsakov (rim-skee-KOR-sah-kof)
Golliwog's Cakewalk from "Children's Corner Suite"	Debussy (duh-bew-SEE)
Hall of the Mountain King from "Peer Gynt Suite"	Grieg (greeg)
Little Train from "Once Upon a Time Suite"	Donaldson (DON-uld-son)
Little White Donkey	Ibert (ee-BEAR)
March of the Royal Lion from "Carnival of the Animals"	Saint-Saens (seh-SAW)
Three Bears	Coates (kohtz)
Viennese Musical Clock from "Hary Janos Suite"	Kodaly (koh-DALL-yee)

*Suggested listening selections are from "Music Guide for Arizona Elementary Schools," Department of Public Instruction, 1964. Used by permission.

The following rules of pronunciation apply: Composer's names are respelled phonetically without diacritical markings. Each syllable should be pronounced as it appears in terms of usual English word sounds. Capital letters indicate accented syllables.

3. *Marches*

Selection	Composer
Funeral March of the Marionettes	Gounod (goo-NO)
March from "The Love of Three Oranges"	Prokofiev (proh-KOH-fee-ef)
March from "The Nutcracker Suite"	Tchaikovsky (ch-eye-KOFF-skee)
March of the Dwarfs	Grieg (greeg)
March of the Little Lead Soldiers	Pierne (pee-er-NAY)
March of the Siamese Children from "The King and I"	Rodgers (ROD-jers)
March of the Toys from "Babes in Toyland"	Herbert (HER-burt)
Parade	Ibert (ee-BEAR)
Pomp and Circumstance No. 1	Elgar (EL-gar)
Stars and Stripes Forever	Sousa (SOO-sah)

4. *Dances*

Selection	Composer
Anitra's Dance from "Peer Gynt Suite"	Grieg (greeg)
Dance of the Sugarplum Fairy from "The Nutcracker Suite"	Tchaikovsky (ch-eye-KOFF-skee)
Dance of the Toy Flutes from "The Nutcracker Suite"	Tchaikovsky (ch-eye-KOFF-skee)
Petite Ballerina from "Ballet Suite No. 1"	Shostakovich (shah-stuh-KOH-vich)
Skater's Waltz	Waldteufel (val-toy-FELL)
Sleeping Beauty Waltz from "Sleeping Beauty Ballet"	Tchaikovsky (ch-eye-KOFF-skee)
Waltz of the Doll from "Coppelia"	Delibes (duh-LEEB)
Waltz of the Flowers from "The Nutcracker Suite"	Tchaikovsky (ch-eye-KOFF-skee)

Singing

Books

Aubin, E., and others, *Silver Burdett Music: Early Childhood.* Morristown, NJ: Silver Burdett/General Learning Corporation, 1976.

Birkenshaw, L., *Music for Fun, Music for Learning,* 2d ed. NY: Holt, Rinehart and Winston, 1978.

Bitcon, C., *Alike and Different.* 18361 Whitney Dr., Santa Ana, CA.; Rosha Press, 1976.

Boardman, E., B. Landis, and B. Andress, *Exploring Music, Kindergarten.* NY: Holt, Rinehart and Winston, 1975.

Bradford, L., *Sing It Yourself: 220 Pentatonic Folk Songs.* NY: Alfred Music Company, 1978.

Choate, R., and others, *Music for Early Childhood: New Dimensions in Music.* NY: American Book Company, 1976.

Marsh, M., C. Rinehart, and E. Savage, *The Spectrum of Music: Kindergarten Book.* NY: Macmillan Publishing Company 1974.

McLaughlin, R., and L. Wood, *The Small Singer.* Glendale, CA: Bowmar Publication Corporation, 1969.

Nash, G., *Today with Music.* NY: Alfred Music Company, 1978.

Nash, G., and others, *Do It My Way.* NY: Alfred Music Company, 1977.

Regner, H., and others, *Music for Children, Primary, Vol. 2.* NY: Schott Music Corporation, 1977.

Wood, L., and R. McLaughlin, *Sing a Song of Holidays and Seasons.* Glendale, CA: Bowmar Publication Corporation, 1969.

Wood, L., and L. Scott, *More Singing Fun.* St. Louis, MO: Webster Publishing Company, 1961.

Wood, L., and L. Scott, *Singing Fun.* St. Louis, MO: Webster Publishing Company, 1954.

Recordings and Accompanying Books

McLaughlin, R., and L. Wood, *The Small Singer.* Glendale, CA: Bowmar Records.

Wood, L., and R. McLaughlin, *Sing a Song of Holidays and Seasons.* Glendale, CA: Bowmar Records.

Wood, L., and L. Scott, *Singing Fun and More Singing Fun.* Glendale, CA: Bowmar Records.

Sound-making Objects

Books

Biasini, A., R. Thomas, and L. Pogonowsky, *MMCP Interaction— Early Childhood Music Curriculum.* Bardonia, NY: Media Materials, 1965.

Burton, L., and others, *Music Play.* Menlo Park, CA: Addison-Wesley Publishing Company, 1979.

Evans, D., *Sharing Sounds.* NY: Longman Group, 1978.

Records*

1. *Quiet Listening*

Selection	Composer
Air for G String from "Suite No. 3 in D Major"	Bach (bahk)

Aquarium from "Carnival of the Animals"	Saint-Saens (seh-SAW)
Barcarolle from "Tales of Hoffman"	Offenbach (OFF-fen-bahk)
Berceuse from "The Firebird Suite"	Stravinsky (strah-VIN-skee)
Clair de Lune	Debussy (duh-bew-SEE)
Lullaby	Brahms (brahmz)
Morning from "Peer Gynt Suite"	Grieg (greeg)
The Swan from "Carnival of the Animals"	Saint-Saens (seh-SAW)
Traumerei	Schumann (SHOO-mahn)

2. *Additional Listening*

Selection	Composer
Andante from "Surprise Symphony"	Haydn (HIDE-n)
Carnival of the Animals	Saint-Saens (seh-SAW)
Children's Corner Suite	Debussy (duh-bew-SEE)
Children's Symphony, (Third Movement)	McDonald (mac-DON-uld)
Mother Goose Suite	Ravel (rah-VELL)
Nutcracker Suite	Tchaikovsky (ch-eye-KOFF-skee)
Peer Gynt Suite	Grieg (greeg)
Peter and the Wolf	Prokofiev (proh-KOH-fee-ef)
Toy Symphony	Haydn (HIDE-n)

Method Books

Carley, I., *Recorder Improvisation and Technique, Book One.* Brasstown, NC: Brasstown Press, 1978.

Nash, G., *Music with Children, Series I, II, III Recorder Book.* Scottsdale, AZ: G.C. Nash, 1965.

Orr, H., *Basic Recorder Technique, Volume 1-Soprano.* NY: Associated Music Publishers, Inc., 1969.

Sevush, L., *Let's Play Recorder, Level 1.* Milwaukee, WI: Hal Leonard Publishing Corporation, 1973.

Snyder, J., *Basic Instructor Guitar, I, II.* NY: Charles Hansen Distributor, 1976.

*Suggested selections from "Music Guide for Arizona Elementary Schools," Department of Public Instruction, 1964. Used by permission.

Teacher Skills

Guitar Chords

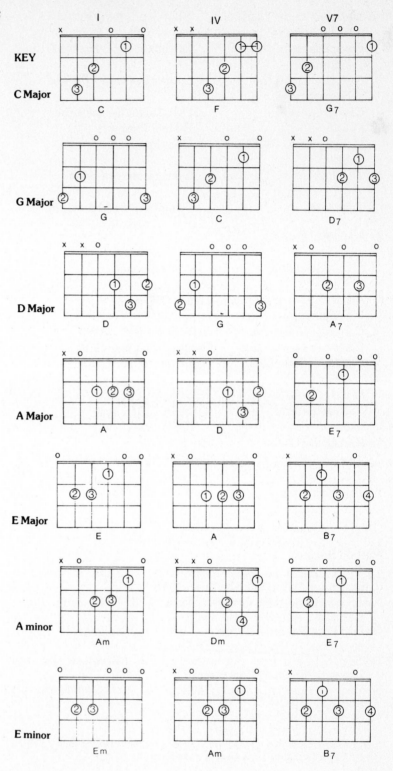

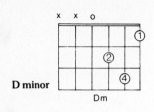
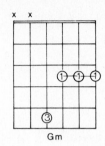
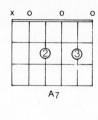

D minor

Dm

Gm

A7

Melody: *Rock-a-My Soul* (verse only)

Beginning Pitch: F# Key of D

Words

Do this, my friend,
Just-a-like me

Do this, my friend,
Just-a-like-me

Do this, my friend,
Just-a-like me,

Oh_____ just-a-like me.

(Move with the beat)
  clap
  stamp
  sway
pat knees or floor

(point to self)

Melody: *Good News*

Beginning pitch: A Key of F

Words

Hello! Look who's here now,
Hello! Look who's here now,
Hello! Look who's here now,
(Ronnie's) here today!

Use names of different children. Teacher points to child on word "Look," finally saying name in last phrase.

Melody *The Farmer in the Dell*

Beginning Pitch: C Key of F

Words

Oh,   if you're wearing tennies (sneakers)
    If you're wearing tennies
    You may walk right out the door
    If you're wearing tennies.

Songs to Use Throughout the Day

New Words to Familiar Tunes

Oh,   If you're wearing brown shoes . . . .

Oh,   If you're wearing blue jeans . . . .

Melody *Skip To My Lou* (refrain only)

Beginning pitch: F# Key of D

Words

Walk! Walk! Walk to the circle,
Walk! Walk! Walk to the circle,
Walk! Walk! Walk to the circle,
Walk to the circle now.

Sit! Sit! Sit in the circle . . . .

Stand! Stand! . . .

Melody *The Work Song* (excerpt) from Snow White and the Seven Dwarfs

Beginning Pitch: C Key of F

Words

Hey, ho! Hey, ho!
It's clean up time, you know.
We put each thing right in its place
Hey, ho! Hey, Ho! Ho! Ho! Ho! . . .

(Improvise "ho" melody as we work or repeat the song several times)

RESTING TIME SONGS

Resting

Slowly, softly

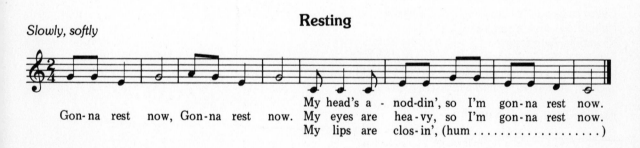

Gon-na rest   now, Gon-na rest   now. My head's a - nod-din', so I'm gon-na rest   now.
My eyes are   hea-vy, so I'm gon-na rest   now.
My lips are   clos-in', (hum . . . .)

Bell Accompaniment

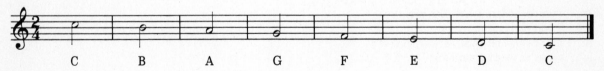

C   B   A   G   F   E   D   C

By-lo-li-lee

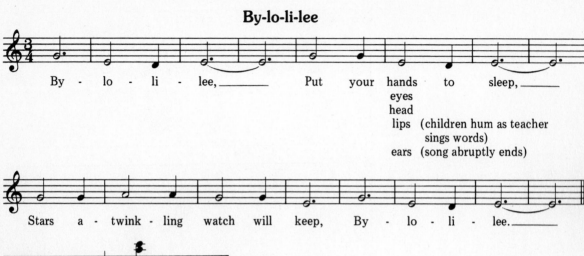

By - lo - li - lee, _____ Put your hands to sleep, _____
eyes
head
lips (children hum as teacher sings words)
ears (song abruptly ends)

Stars a - twink - ling watch will keep, By - lo - li - lee. _____

Guitar

Read story. Play sounds at appropriate times. You may wish to use the pictures in a flannel board story or prepare picture cards that present the story in sequence.

Enrichment Materials

A "SOUND" STORY

Old Mr. Wind
Was as clumsy as could be.
He was always getting in trouble
And He'd sigh, "Oh, my! Oh, me!"

He blew in Mrs. Murphy's window
And broke her favorite cup

Then he whirled around the floor
And snaggled her kitten up!

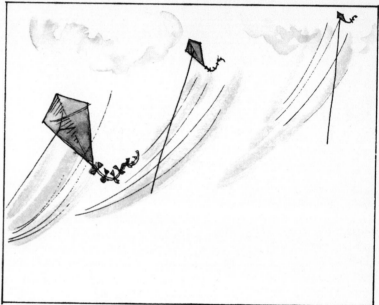

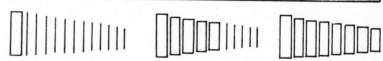

But when he blew at Johnny,
Johnny said, "That just isn't right!
From now on I'll keep you busy,
You'll help me fly my kite."

So Mr. Wind started
Way low on the ground
He blew higher and higher
And proudly waved the kite around.

Then he blew the kite
Til it reached up so high
That all there was left
Was a speck in the sky!

MUSIC MANIPULATIVES

INSTRUCTIONS: Trace figures on pellon (available at fabric shops). Use colored felt pens. Cut two of each sketch (front with pattern; back plain fabric). Sew around edges before cutting out. Use the "Singer" finger puppets to motivate improvised songs of children.

Bibliography

Andress, B., and others, *Music in Early Childhood.* Washington, D.C.: Music Educators National Conference, 1973.

Aronoff, F., *Music and Young Children.* NY: Holt, Rinehart and Winston, 1969.

Aronoff, F., "No Age is Too Early to Begin," *Music Educators Journal 60,* March 1974.

Biasini, A., R. Thomas, and L. Pogonowsky, *MMCP Interaction—Early Childhood Music Curriculum.* Bardonia, NY: Media Materials, 1965.

Birkenshaw, L., *Music for Fun, Music for Learning,* 2d ed. NY: Holt, Rinehart and Winston, 1978.

Bitcon, C., *Alike and Different.* 18361 Whitney Dr. Santa Ana, CA: Rosha Press, 1976.

Boardman, E., B. Landis, and B. Andress, *Exploring Music, Kindergarten.* NY: Holt, Rinehart and Winston, 1975.

Boardman, E., "An Investigation of the Effect of Preschool Training on the Development of Vocal Accuracy in Young Children." Unpublished dissertation, University of Illinois, 1964.

Caplan, F., and T. Caplan, *The Power of Play.* NY: Anchor Press/ Doubleday, 1973.

Cherry, C., *Creative Movement for the Developing Child,* 2d ed. Belmont, CA: Fearon-Pitman Publishers, 1971.

Cherry, C., *Creative Play for the Developing Child.* Belmont, CA: Fearon-Pitman Publishers, 1976.

Chukovsky, K., *From Two to Five.* Berkeley, CA: University of California Press, 1963.

Erikson, E., *Childhood and Society,* rev. ed. NY: W.W. Norton & Company, 1964.

Fowler, W., "Cognitive Learning in Infancy and Early Childhood." *Psychological Bulletin LIX* (1962).

Fridman, R., "The First Cry of the Newborn: Basis for Child's Future

Musical Development." *Journal of Research in Music Education,* 21, Fall 1973.

Simons, G. Follow-Through Research Report: Early Childhood Musical Development". (A bibliography of Research Abstracts 1960-73). University of Georgia, Athens. Georgia 30602.

Zimmerman, M., *Musical Characteristics of Children.* Washington, D.C.: Music Educators National Conference, 1971.

Zimmerman, M., and Seechrest, "How Children Conceptually Organize Sounds." Washington D.C.: Cooperative Research Project No. 5-0256, 1968.

Identifying and Developing Music Behaviors: A Design for Learning. Arizona Department of Education, 1973.

Readings on the Learning Process

Ayres, A., *Sensory Integration and Learning Disorders.* Los Angeles, CA: Manson Western Corporation, 1972.

Bogen, J., "The Other Side of the Brain, II: An appositional mind," *Bulletin of the Los Angeles Neurological Society,* 34, 1969.

Bogen, J., and G. Bogen, "The Other Side of the Brain III: The corpus callosum and creativity," *Bulletin of the Los Angeles Neurological Society,* 34, 1969.

Bruner, J., *Toward a Theory of Instruction.* Cambridge, MA: Harvard University Press, 1971.

Lavatelli, C., *Paget's Theory Applied to an Early Childhood Curriculum.* Boston, MA: American Science and Engineering, 1970.

Lee, P. and others, *Symposium on Consciousness.* NY: Viking Press, 1976.

Litchtenberg, P., Norton, D. *Cognitive and Mental Development in the First Five Years of Life.* National Institute of Mental Health, 1970. Rockville, Maryland.

Maccheroni, A., *Developing the Music Senses.* Cincinnati, OH: Greenwood Press, World Library, 1950.

Miller, J., *Music Theory with the Bells in a Montessori Environment.* Cincinnati, OH: Montessori Development Foundation, 1970.

Montessori, M., *Dr. Montessori's Own Handbook.* NY: Schocken Books, 1976.

Montessori, M., *The Montessori Elementary Material, Vol. 2.* NY: Schocken Books, 1973.

Montessori, M., Jr., *Education for Human Development.* NY: Schocken Books, 1976.

Morrison, G., *Early Childhood Education Today.* Columbus, OH: Merrill Publishers, 1976.

Ornstein, R., *The Psychology of Consciousness.* NY: Penguin Books, 1975.

Piaget, J., *Play, Dreams, and Imitation in Childhool.* NY: W. W. Norton Company, 1962.

Piaget, J., and B. Inhelder, *The Psychology of the Child.* NY: Basic Books, 1969.

Phillips, J., Jr., *The Origins of Intellect: Piaget's Theory.* San Francisco, CA: W. H. Freeman and Company, 1975.

Rose, S., *The Conscious Brain.* NY: Random House, 1976.

Serafine, M., "A measure of meter conservation in music, based on Piaget's theory, "Ph.D. dissertation, University of Florida, 1975.

Standing, E., *The Montessori Revolution in Education*. NY: Schocken Books, 1966.

Wadsworth, B., *Piaget's Theory of Cognitive Development*. NY: David McKay Company, 1974.

Wittrock, M., The Human Brain. Englewood Cliffs, NJ: Prentice Hall, 1977.

Index

SONG TITLE INDEX